Bolloxology

Also by Colm O'Regan

Isn't It Well for Ye? The Book of Irish Mammies

That's More of It Now:
The Second Book of Irish Mammies

It's Earlier 'Tis Getting:
The Christmas Book of Irish Mammies

Bolloxology

Colm O'Regan

with cartoons by Twisteddoodles

TRANSWORLD IRELAND

TRANSWORLD IRELAND
28 Lower Leeson Street, Dublin 2, Ireland
www.transworldireland.ie

Transworld Ireland is part of the Penguin Random House group of companies
whose addresses can be found at global.penguinrandomhouse.com

First published in the UK and Ireland by Transworld Ireland
an imprint of Transworld Publishers

A CIP catalogue record for this book
is available from the British Library.

ISBN 9781848272286

Typeset in 11.25/16 pt Serifa by Jouve (UK), Milton Keynes
Printed and bound in Great Britain by Clays Ltd, Bungay, Suffolk

Penguin Random House is committed to a sustainable
future for our business, our readers and our planet. This book
is made from Forest Stewardship Council® certified paper.

5 7 9 10 8 6

Contents

Part Three: Social

Introduction

First and Foremost, Before I Answer, Can I Just Say . . .

BOLLOXOLOGY – we've all heard the word and once you hear it you remember it. It contains a number of pleasing /ɒ/ sounds as all the best words do, like 'toss', 'nob' and 'How are ya, HORSE?' But what does it *mean*?

It's a very powerful word, a useful gateway into understanding modern Ireland. Think of it as being a combination of bullshit, codology and oul talk. It's infused with a subtle blend of notions, a touch of misplaced arrogance and smidgens of devilment.

The word itself sounds a little condemnatory but it needn't be. Don't worry – we all indulge in a spot of bolloxology. Doing something bolloxological doesn't make you a bollox, just like engaging in codology does not make you a deep-sea North Atlantic fish. But it's important to be able to identify it when presented to you.

Bolloxology can take many forms. It may be about

getting served your ice-cream in a restaurant *on a piece of slate.* Or worse – the restaurant having no ice-cream at all on the menu (known as bolloxology by omission). Luckily, the average Irish person has an inbuilt sixth sense for bolloxology. You know that slight rage you feel when you read an article entitled '25 IRISH CELEBRITIES WHO ARE "KILLING IT" ON INSTAGRAM RIGHT NOW'? That's not future-shock. That's your bolloxological sensor going off.

Notions lie at the root of much bolloxology. For many Irish people, notions were once synonymous with having 'notions above your station'. But that was a harsh definition, condemning any ordinary person for just trying to inject a bit of happiness in their lives with a nice jaunty hat or a non-black bicycle. Now it has been reclaimed from that classist origin. Notions today can range from a hairdresser giving you balayage when all you wanted was 'a tidy', to buying evoting machines that were never used.

But notions are not necessarily bad. If you didn't have notions about your station, you would never aspire to get to another station and the basis of the economy would collapse. Where would we be if Isaac Newton, Albert Einstein and Steve Jobs hadn't had notions?

But when those notions lose the run of themselves, allied with the bad data supplied from bolloxological assumptions, disaster can strike – namely, a hames.

This book has a *bit* of language in it. There's a section on bad language but we won't labour the point. And it's well marked with asterisks.

For shorthand, bolloxology is sometimes written as Bx. This is just to spare you from having to stare at a load of bollox all the way through the book. You'll also see a bit of anti-Bx – the antidotes to bolloxology which help deflate some of the nonsense that might be flying around. But there's more Bx than anti-Bx – otherwise we'd have nothing to complain about.

At the end of the book, you will find the Bollexicon – a glossary of a few words and phrases that have seeped into our brains over the last while. If there comes a day when you open your mouth and one of these bits of Bx comes out, the Bollexicon should help you head them off at the pass. You will also meet the Humans of Bolloxology – some representatives of all of us with our funny little ways and notions.

Private. Public. Social.

Bolloxology is inescapable. Take this book, for example: even its very structure is bolloxological. In homage to the three-word slogan (see page 188) it is divided into three main sections:

- **Private** – how we talk and carry on among ourselves.

- **Public** – how we talk and carry on in the full glare of the public eye.

3

- **Social** – how we talk and carry on as if we were talking and carrying on among ourselves but are apparently unaware that, because it's on social media, it's actually in the full glare of the public eye.

Of course, language, behaviour and attitudes are fluid across many different categories. For example, the unique grammar of the English-speaking Irish is like a horizontal that transcends all the major verticals of the book. But mention of horizontals and verticals is exactly the kind of Bx that has led to the demands for this book to be written.

However, in honour of the bolloxology at the heart of the political system, we went with an imperfect solution to 'get the thing out the door' before the next election because our focus groups were telling us we needed to 'shore up the grass roots'. And if it comes back to bite us, sure 'twon't be me that'll be dealing with it. I'll be gone to Europe to take up a new job and claim a pension simultaneously. Or else I'll have taken up a job in sports administration – which appears to be a hotbed of Bx.

"WHAT DID YOU GET UP TO ON SATURDAY NIGHT?"

PRIVATE

CLOSE FRIEND

PUBLIC

BOSS

SOCIAL

BEST NITE EVA!! #YOLO
#STUNHUN #SESHMOTH

Mammy's Introduction

Time to Move On

WHEN I HEARD HE WAS WRITING another book I thought to myself, What is he going to be telling people about me now? So, to tell you the truth, I'm glad he's moved on from writing about me. Three books is more than enough to be giving away our secrets. I can't go anywhere now without someone saying, *Oh, the Irish Mammy does this* and *the Irish Mammy does that*, when all I'm trying to do is buy a few spare tea-towels. Everything I do now seems to end up in some sort of a list. And I normally would be a great one for a list but not when I'm an item on it.

Now, as regards this book . . . I might as well come out and say it: I'm not sure about the language – *especially on the cover.* He tells me that it's not a big deal now to say it but I think myself it's only looking for attention. Exactly, Mammy, he says – you need to grab their attention in the bookshop. Well, says I, there's *no need* to be crude. And then there's more bad language further in. They've put in stars but I know the words they're talking about, and again . . . there's plenty of ways of saying something without resorting to that sort of thing.

But lookit, I spose he has to make a shilling out of something. The car insurance went up again, he tells me, even though he still has the no-claims bonus. 'Tis all them scam artists with their 'whiplash'. I heard about it on *Prime Time*.

And the thing is, he's old enough now to go his own way so if he wants to talk about bolloxism or whatever it's called, leave him off. But I probably won't leave the book lying around the house in case visitors would see it. There'd be a few On My Side who would have fairly strong opinions about that kind of a thing.

Part One

PRIVATE

1

There IS a Need for That Kind of Language

MUCH HAS BEEN WRITTEN about Hiberno-English. A lot of it has been immense works of scholarship, cross-referencing old texts, researching etymologies and making links with Indo-European languages and whatnot. This has not been done here, though it *totally* could have been, and anyway, in today's busy world, who has time for that? Instead it's just broad strokes and generalizations. That'll do you grand.

The way we speak here in Ireland is a sometimes entertaining mix of our natural bent towards bolloxology and our natural resistance to it.

Years of oppression by the Tuatha Dé Danann, the Vikings, the Normans, the English, ourselves, the Church, the professional classes, the banks, the EU and finally, our phones, have had a number of effects:

• We equivocate a lot. It is difficult to give a straight answer because we're not sure who's asking. This vagueness in the detail can also come back to bite us when organizing a large public project and may ultimately lead to a hames (see page 170).

• We can be excessively modest – not taking any credit for anything, even if it was clearly proven we did it. Although we will take huge amounts of credit to buy a house at the wrong time in an economic cycle.

• There's a chance the person asking the question might be able to pay good money for the answer. Over the years, these lucrative questioners have ranged from Redcoats with shiny sovereigns asking about 'which blacksmith seems to be up the walls making pikes these days' to successful businessmen idly wondering 'how's that competition for the big wedge of public money going, would you say?' In such cases, a particular and indirect form of words is required. This is usually prefaced with the phrase 'Well, you didn't hear this from me now . . .'

Finally, as a small country, we are also very open to language coming in from abroad. Our social survival depends on it, in much the same way as our economy depends on our openness to huge organizations that earn billions but pay €14.25 and a packet of Monster Munch in tax. But from time to time we have enough of

Bx and explode in a beautiful stream of good 'bad language' with a grammar all of its own.

Here is a quick tour of the Irish argot and how the Bx or anti-Bx applies.

You Say It Best When You Say Nothing at All (at All)

When we don't have enough words to fill the available space, we use a lot of filler words. These are innocuous enough in private conversation but when taken into the more public sphere, they're usually a sign we're hiding something – like the truth or the fact that we don't know our arse from our elbow.

Filler words are also used when we don't want a sentence to start too abruptly or, more importantly, when we're trying to avoid saying something else. They can soften a blow, calm an argument or deflect a difficult question. They are a buffer zone of language.

Before I say another word

I suppose/I spose
The popularity of 'I suppose' is new-found, although its use is not. We've been 'sposing' for years. On occasion, 'I spose' has been abbreviated to the ultra-efficient 'I boz' and appears at the end of a sentence. The finest exponents are farmers standing in a field and

conjecturing about the progress of a man driving heavy machinery. 'He'll hardly do both fields before the rain, I boz.'

Some advanced-level users will place it at the beginning *and* end of a sentence. 'I boz the digger'll hardly go through that gate, I boz.' To which the reply is 'I boz not'.

I suppose, to be fair though, 'I suppose' has made the leap from the gate of a field to many other fields and now peppers the speech of even the most erudite of speakers.

Sports people spend a lot of post-match interviews 'supposing', as a way of avoiding saying that they won because they were better than their opponents. Given that they suppose about the past, you can imagine how much supposing there is about the future. For example, the All-Ireland Final preview programmes, *Up for the Match*, are almost two-thirds pure supposition.

Look/Lookit

Often used in conjunction with 'I suppose', 'lookit' was originally the domain of an exasperated Mammy who was just telling the youngest to wear *some* sort of a coat as it was freezing out. Now you can hear it from any GAA manager who is being asked to speculate on his opponents in the next round. 'Lookit, we'll look at our own game first and I'm sure Kilkenny will do the same.'

We'll explore this more deeply in the sports section

(see page 95), but the reason for so many 'I sposes' and 'lookits' is pure bolloxology: sports people simply don't like talking about sport, and sports broadcasters keep wanting to interview them to fill the hours of time set aside in the broadcast schedule for analysis and preview.

So

The way 'so' is used now has seeped in from abroad. It has always had lots of uses but, in the past, it would appear in the middle of a flow of conversation. For example:

- As part of the phrase 'so that was grand'. STWG is used to connect two events in a long anecdote even if the events themselves were anything but grand. 'He drove straight through the window, nearly up as far as the deli counter. So that was grand. Then the father came in and he was balubas as well and caught his hand on a pane of glass.'

- In recounting a 'he says/I says' conversation with optional turning around. 'No,' he says. So I turned around and says, 'Well, you can shove your golf-night up your hole, so.'

It has now been imported to the beginning of a conversation. Sometimes it's in a 'look-at-me' statement: 'So I'm single again.' This is a plea for attention, but the 'so' indicates that the pleader is being a real trooper about the whole thing. IT professionals use it to soften the blow when explaining complex concepts to idiots. 'So, yeah, if you just click on "OK" then that should work' or 'So the plug goes in the wall.' Irish politicians use 'so' to demonstrate their dynamism, in whatever sort-of solution they are proposing: 'So, we've set up a task force and they'll be meeting in 2018.'

Dhera/Arra/Musha/Wisha/Ah shur

Used to express a lack of surprise that what has transpired has confirmed our suspicion that we were right to have such low expectations. 'Dhera, they were in trouble for ages. Someone said he was into the bank for a good few bob.'

Like

The oldest ones are the best. 'Like' is one of these words. It's been around for years, particularly in Cork, where it's used as a substitute for breathing. Coincidentally, it also originated in the San Fernando Valley in California. But whereas the Valley Girl was 'like, whatever', the Cork girl was '*like, allergic*'. A typical conversation might include the following: 'Like, I don't know, like, if he likes me or not, like, like he liked my Facebook status, like, but like, that could mean anything, like.'

Asking for confirmation that the listener knows what you are talking about

Some of these fillers may have been quite long phrases at one stage but over time have become fused together like a load of sticky old sweets in a bag at the back of the press.

- 'Do you know' becomes 'jnaw'.

- 'Do you know what I mean' becomes 'janoreamean' in Dublin; while it has been further condensed in the countryside to 'jahmean', which sounds like a Rastafarian cursing his Creator's cruelty.

Just words, we're not sure why they're there

Now

You never need tell the Irish retail and food industry to live in the present. They do it all the time. Even if they're just setting a plate down on a restaurant table or 'getting a size ten in the black', there is an involuntary 'now'. 'Now' is short for 'Here is the thing that you ordered. I have delivered it to you.'

It turns out that we all learned it from our parents. New parents will realize for the first time that the main use for filler words is to say something to a baby who is just staring at you like you are an idiot and they are debating whether or not to send a message to the home planet to beam them back up. That's when we say 'now' to a baby.

Sorry

For a country much wronged against, we do spend a lot of time apologizing profusely for some/all of the following situations, and many others besides:

- Not holding a door for someone even though they were outside the 'holding zone'.

- Buying something in a shop with mainly coins, dropping the coins, in the end just changing your mind and handing over the €50 note, even though you *definitely* had €13.50 in coins because you counted it out in the biscuit aisle.

- When you are about to complain about terrible service, all the way through complaining about terrible service and even after you've been granted an inadequate recompense for terrible service.

Ironically, 'sorry now' is quite powerful: 'Sorry now, excuse me, but that kind of behaviour is NOT acceptable. What did we say? Exactly. Well, we're going straight home and you won't be going to Funwaterworld again until you learn to behave.'

Private Parts of Speech

There are times when we've had enough of Bx. There are times when the enabling, the empowering and the envisioning have to be dissed, when the *key drivers* have to be run off the road, when those *reaching out* need to have their hands slapped. When the Irish snap, the language is bold and beautiful. Most of the bold words are asterisked out here so that the book doesn't get a parental advisory sticker on the cover. This in itself is a load of Bx. It's supposed to protect children. These are the same children who are browsing in the bookshop for a novel about a post-apocalyptic world where all the parents are dead and the children have to fight to save the human race from a nameless evil. These are the same children who'll have all the worst words and who laugh into their sleeves when you look up from reading about a court-case and say, 'I don't understand; what's the big deal with teabagging? I mean it's not as nice as loose tea but still . . . Although I don't understand why they'd be doing it in a jeep.'

Anyway, we asterisked the offending words out just to be on the safe side. Because when we get annoyed, we get some new grammar – a huge body of grammar.

The biological voices

Assign a body part to complete the following phrases.
(Please note that there may be more than one correct answer).

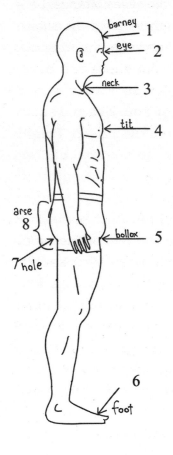

a) 'I will in my _____'
b) 'He has some _____ on him to try that.'
c) 'Don't bother your _____.'
d) 'They've made a right _____ of it'.
e) 'Ask me _____.'
f) 'Shove it up your _____.'
g) 'I'll shove me _____ up your _____ in a minute if you don't stop that carry on.'

Answers: (a) 2, 5, 6 or 7; (b) 3; (c) 1 or 7; (d) 4; (e) 5 or 7; (f) 7 or 8; (g) 6 and 7.

A *fierce selection of intensifiers*

It should be in the guide books, really. We have a lot of words for 'very' and a lot of them would be unexpected to tourists. To avoid confusion, or in some cases offence, here are most of them in one place: mighty, fierce, ferocious, savage, quare, fair, wile, wicked, dead, awful, terrible, massive, pure. The bolloxology is that these are being eroded by Americanisms such as 'soooo', 'waayyy' and the one that causes me to whiten my knuckles and shout into a cushion: 'much'. As in 'Overreacting much, Colm?'

Curses, foiled again

You could write a whole book about Irish swearing with a hundred pages devoted to the use of the word 'f*ck' alone – a word we have embraced very keenly. We could deal with the c-word as well but it would be nice to have some chance of getting this book discussed on afternoon telly, so that chapter will be left to *Bolloxology Redux* – a handsome, leather-bound edition costing a huge amount of money that contains very little you didn't already know from the copy you got in the library.

The main contribution to the pantheon of f*ck from this part of the world is 'to f*ck'. Its incredible prevalence would suggest the Irish are getting a savage amount of sex but actually it's just a replacement for other words or a full stop. In this context, when used at the end of a sentence 'to f*ck' means to a non-specific location that isn't the current location. It is often used as a response to 'f*ck-acting around' (a physical form of bolloxology characterized by a lack of efficiency and directness in one's actions).

Examples include: 'C'mon away to f*ck'/'Gway to f*ck'/'Leh ih inta f*ck' – the last being a supporter's plea for a fancy dan footballer to cut out the fancy dan stuff and send the ball into 'the mixer' in a more timely fashion.

'To f*ck' is sometimes just used for the f*ck of it. Honest to f*ck it is. Anyway, we'll carry on to the next section, to f*ck.[1]

Continuous interrogative

One of the key features of Irish-English is that it is spoken by people who are cautious – especially men. For Irish men, the hardest thing to do is greet another man face-on. Therefore, the initial few minutes of any interaction have to contain absolutely nothing in the line of information. This is a prime example of bolloxology by omission, as the following conversation shows:

Man 1: 'Well . . .'

Man 2: 'How are you?'

Man 1: 'How're things?'

[1] One 'false friend' in Hiberno-English is specific to Northern Hiberno-English where 'f*ck up' means 'shut up' whereas down south it means 'a mistake'. In theory, in a united Ireland you could order someone to 'f*ck up about the f*ck-up' but that's a long way off.

Man 2: 'How'd ye get on?'

Man 1: 'Ah . . . shur, you know yourself.'

Man 2: 'Shur, who are ya tellin'?'

This could go on for another few minutes unless there is another action to be performed:

Man 1: 'Pint?'

Man 2: 'F*ckitgwanso.'

Or another person enters the group – although the ritual may have to be repeated:

Man 3: 'How're the men?'

Man 1/Man 2: 'Ah, would ya look who it is?'

Man 3: 'Hard at it, are ye?'

Man 1: 'What would you know about hard work?'

The silent voice

The silent voice is what is *really* meant by what is actually said. It's like a dog whistle for humans but instead of a high-pitched sound, it's those unspoken words directed at you and your oul talk.

An emigrant coming back

The conversation between a returned emigrant and the person who stayed can be laden with subtext, with neither side saying overtly what they want to say, *even though they may be screaming inside*, as the following example shows:

'I thought it was you, all right. Well, how're you getting on – over in LA, is it?'

'San Fran, actually.' *He knows well where I am. I told him before. Keeps getting it wrong just to show he doesn't give a shite where I am.*

'San Francisco, bedads.' *San Fran he says. F*ckin' San Fran. He's out there two minutes and he has all the lingo now about it.* 'You like it out there?' *I hope he doesn't.*

'Oh yeah. It's just a different world, you know?' *Not a world for the likes of you anyway. With your Penneys polo shirt and your Barratts shoes.*

'Who are you working for? Google or Facebook, I suppose. One a them Silicon Valley crowds, I suppose.' *God, I hope Silicon Valley is in San Francisco.*

'No, you wouldn't have heard of them – Softoid. But we're on the same campus, actually. All part of one ecosystem.' *Why did I say 'ecosystem', feck's sake? That'll be all over the parish by* tomorrow. *I'll have to replatform my language. [Laughs internally]*

'Eco-system'? *The clown — always was full of it.* 'Softoid. I don't know them. Must be a small crowd, are they? Wan a them start-ups?' *Probably fly-by-nights. Thank f*ck he's not with Google. I'd never hear the end of it from the father. Shur, I know what he was doing — wasn't I looking up the photos on Facebook of him going around in a driverless car or whatever the f*ck.*

'Actually it's got a market cap of thirty billion but it's very much under the radar. But you'll hear about it, I'd say, when it IPOs. The CAPEX on our B2B model for SMEs is attracting a lot of VC interest. The NASDAQ is going to go nuts for it.' *That's it now. I can never come home again.*

'CAPEX, yeah, they go stone mad for the CAPEX, all right.' *The tool.* 'You must be on big money out there.' *I hope he's not but I know he is. Tell us how many shares you're getting. Go on, put us out of our misery.*

'Haha. It's a good living. But you know, long hours so . . . Would you not think of going out there yourself?' *If you can tear yourself away from Saturday nights in O'Dwyers.*

'Ah, no. Wouldn't be for the likes of me.' *I'm fine*

and happy where I am, or at least I was until you walked in.

'I'd say you'd like it. It's real active. We go skiing every weekend in the winter and then it's a short drive to the ocean for surfing. It's not just staying in the pub.' *I just want you to approve of what I'm doing, it's not a competition. Well, maybe it is actually. You thought you were the dog's bollox when we were seventeen. Well, who's winning now?*

'Skiing. Begor. There won't be much skiing for me now anyway with the young lads, haha. Have you family yourself out there?'

'No.' *He wins that one anyway. Can't compete with having a family.*

'Ah shur – plenty of time, I suppose.' *Well, at least I'm married and have a family and built a house and stayed around and am putting in the hard yards in the community and doing all the dull stuff while you're stuck out there with a load of humourless Yanks going skiing with some f*cker who won't know your name next year when he goes off to work with some other shower that make some other internet thing. And you'll be fifty, sitting at some barbecue going on about sidewalks and the trunk of your car and you'll be just as boring as me, but with a better tan.*

'I suppose so.' *C'mon away out so and we'll have*

the craic. *I'll show you all around Castro on Pride weekend and you'll never have seen anything like it in your life.*

'Good man.' *Probably gay himself, I'd say. They all are out in San Francisco. I wonder what it's like, though?*

'And how are things here?' *Go on, tell me how bad it is. It keeps me going, reading all the comments on the Indo website with people moaning.*

'Goin' well, actually.' *I'm not going to give HIM the satisfaction of telling him anything's wrong anyway.*

'So that's the way now.' *I'd love to spend six months at home.*

'That's the way.' *I'd love to spend six months out there.*

2

Bolloxology, Thy Name Is Progress

'OBVIOUSLY THERE WILL be some teething difficulties but you'll start to see huge efficiencies once the system has bedded down. It will optimize existing processes,' they say. 'There will be increasing convenience for customers and exciting new opportunities will come on stream.' The modern world brings with it the prospect of progress. We are promised a brave new world, or a safer, more secure world. But progress also brings with it a load of oul shite.

Wrong on Queue

Humans are hard work at the best of times, but you'll miss them when they're gone.

Take the stealthy takeover of self-service. We didn't notice it at first. Filling our own petrol tanks? Sure, why not. Getting our own sausages – and sometimes making our own pancakes – at the hotel breakfast bar? It's just as handy. The 'unexpected item in bagging area' woman? Oh, she'd drive you mad but she's only doing her job, I spose. Gradually though, the power of self has spread and now it's in the bank.

There are two layers of security in the average branch. First of all you have to get through their airlock security system and wait for the green light.

The other layer is human. As you walk in, you have to try to sidestep friendly bank staff as they gently remind you of your capabilities. 'Do you want to save time and use the lodgement machine?' is their opening gambit, much as a Jehovah's Witness might ask, 'Would you like to hear about how you can be saved by Jesus Christ?' If you falter at all they will gently guide you to a flashing screen. 'It's great if you want to skip the queue,' they say. You feel like screaming, 'THERE WOULDN'T BE A QUEUE IF YOU WENT BEHIND THE COUNTER' or 'I JUST WANT THE WARM EMBRACE OF A HUMAN VOICE AND TO FEEL LIKE THEY NEED THE UP-TO-DATE INFORMATION I HAVE ON WHAT THE WEATHER IS LIKE OUT THERE NOW.'

But there's no point in giving out to the bank staff. They're just enforcing a policy. It's like visiting someone, only for them to direct you to a screen display in their hall, showing their Facebook page. 'If you're in a hurry,' they say, 'you can check all my news here. It's much faster than waiting for me to boil the kettle and look to see if I've any biscuits.'

When the robots rise and enslave humanity, there

won't be a war like in the *Terminator* movies. The key moment will occur when the banking machines turn sentient. They won't annihilate us, just bamboozle us in the way their human forbears did. They will lock us into a 'range of exciting investment options' which we've no idea how they work and there won't be a thing we can do about it. All because we said we knew how to use the lodgement machine. What else is going to be automated?

Eye in the Sky

You won't know what it is at first – the whirring sound in the air. You'll ignore it and go back to burning rubbish in a barrel in the back yard, or return to your desk by the window to concoct VAT invoices, or upstairs to the Vietnamese lads growing plants in the attic. Or you'll just generally be minding your own business. And then you'll get an email with a link and a hint about paying some money to make this video go away. The whirring sound was a drone and they were recording you.

Sound far-fetched? You won't even have to be up to no good. We used to spy on neighbours through squinting windows; then we went on their Facebook pages. The next frontier is that anyone with €300 to spare will be buying a drone to finally find out what that crowd across the road is building AT ALL out the back.

You won't be able to sunbathe in your underpants – or worse, not in your underpants. No washing line full of raggedy smalls will be safe from scrutiny. It won't be long before you're involved in one of those neighbourhood feuds 'at which Gardaí seized a number of farm implements'.

Drones have other uses. They help media websites fill 20 per cent of their content with videos such as 'Stunning Footage Of Your Local Town As You've Never Seen It Before That Will Have The Tourists Flocking'.

But if everyone has a drone, then the sky will be so full of them that the drone footage will just be of other drones. In which case, you'll have to fly your drone lower and lower to get a clear view of the ground. Still, it doesn't mean we can't get excited about drones and their possibilities.

Record Levels

The surprising stars of the internet in Ireland are the secretly filmed middle and older generations. Mammies having pranks played on them, ould lads roaring at malfunctioning satnavs – all captured for posterity in their natural state, recorded by the country's teens, and twenty- and thirtysomethings.

But eventually, word gets around. The mammy, who was the equivalent of an uncontacted Amazon tribe, is now self-aware. She'll see the phone recording her and say, 'Is this going up online now, is it? Hang on till I change out of this jumper. Would it be funnier if I did it this way? Wait, I'll say that again. Make sure you've enough battery now.'

The Quantum Law of Authenticity (see page 140) has struck.

Studies Say

Right, that's it. We've had enough of studies. There have been a few worthwhile ones in the past but it's getting out of hand now.

We've taken tobacco smoking on board. That's been fairly conclusively proven. And even objectively from a distance one can appreciate that, since smoke from burning plants only occurs naturally as a consequence of volcanic eruptions, lightning and sorcery, chances are humans probably haven't evolved to huff it repeatedly into their lungs without there being some ramifications.

Likewise, eating too much of anything that's made by giant multinationals, who spend millions lobbying American politicians to allow them to put cyanide into a cow's breakfast or something similar, is also likely to be unwise. Because they don't care about whether you get fat or grow a third ear.

But all the other studies? You're better off taking them with a pinch of salt (because you can have salt now, apparently). Anyway, there'll be another study along in a few years that says the first study was wrong because they forgot to carry the four, or the subjects of the study were all found to be complete pint-hounds who were down in McGarrigans every night of the week doing Fat Frogs and bumming fags off the lads in the smoking area.

Life is a study with a thousand variables. The results only come in when you are dead and no one's kept the paperwork, as the Dalai Lama once said. (Well, he didn't but that's the sort of thing he should be saying.)

The straw poll that broke the camel's back came in 2016 with the news that potatoes raise blood pressure. Do you know what really raises blood pressure? Studies that say that potatoes raise blood pressure. Potatoes are bad for you if they're all you eat, the crop fails and it's 1845. If God hadn't wanted us to eat potatoes, he wouldn't have sent the Europeans over to massacre the Indians, copy their menus and get Walter Raleigh to put his coat in front of Queen Elizabeth I so that she'd practically *beg* him to turn East Cork into a farmer's market.

Spuds are still finicky; the turnip is the king of vegetables but you can't eat turnips without spuds. They are the uber-tuber that has launched a thousand chips. We should wash out our mouths with salt for even daring to question them.

So if you hear about a study, ask yourself a few questions:

- How many people did they study?

- Who were they? Where were they? Were they observed or did they report the answers themselves? For example, any study on the sexual habits of teenagers should automatically re-categorize a fella who says he's riding all round him to 'the odd shift now and then'.

- Do the numbers sound suspiciously rounded? 'Thirty-three per cent of people questioned . . .' This probably means they only interviewed three people.

- How did you hear about the study? Was it on a news programme that needed to fill a lot of time during the 'lighter bits' slot? The study industry and the talk industry are wrapped in a deadly embrace of mutual bolloxology.

• Who paid for the research? Clearly the anti-spuds lobby is in the pocket of the quinoa lobby and Big Couscous. Be wary of anything that contains the phrase 'sponsored by'.

Taking the Vapers

The cig is up. Vaping has taken hold. Closed-down bookies have been occupied by premises with catchy names such as Vaper Rooms.

Vaping may help some people quit, and ultimately could help save lives, but at what price? It has robbed smokers of their last dignity, their sense of identity. *Mad Men* with Don Draper sucking on an e-fag just wouldn't have been the same. He may as well have had alcohol-free whiskey in his office and taken a vow of chastity. Whether they're at the bus stop, outside the maternity hospital, the office or freezing in the smoking area (a space at the back of the pub scraped out between empty kegs and the oil tank for the heating), smokers at least *looked* like they were smoking. The last soldiers of a war about to be lost, they still had some sort of uniform, some sort of discipline or ritual. For some, maybe the very act of looking for a light started a relationship, a marriage, a family who, ironically, now beg them to stop smoking and encourage them to take up vaping.

Sure, vaping may hand back a sense of smell, get rid of a smoker's cough, take out the tar and improve health generally, but what about all the things you can't do with one of these jumped-up electro-Bics?

• **Horsing**. To horse a fag is a skill acquired by generations of smokers. It involves taking a hyper-carcinogenic volume of smoke into the lungs, blowing it out through the nose simultaneously, the butt pinched between thumb and index finger, a long string of ash forming on the end of the fag that doesn't even know to fall, such is the hurry. Horsing usually happens in the bike sheds before going back to school after lunch, in the bike sheds before going back into the office after lunch, or just before your bus or train arrives, which brings us to the next lost art . . .

• **Blowing smoke on to public transport**. Yet another bastion of old-fashioned anarchy has fallen; yet another opportunity to stick it to the man has been lost. Taking a giant drag as a bus or tram pulled up, and then blowing it in the door just before it closes was a satisfying way for many to blow smoke in the face of the nanny state. Technically, yes, they'd be blowing smoke into the lungs of non-combatants but this was a war, and passive smokers were just the collateral damage. These days, on seeing the arriving public transport, the vaper can do little more than take a limp puff on their crappy stylus and blow a whimper of steam into the bus, as if they're hiding a tiny kettle in their mouth.

38

• **Smoking a fag without holding it.** The muscular arm of a truck driver with a faded Leeds United FC tattoo on it; the farmer hitting the back of a plough with a wrench for reasons unknown; the harried mother turning right, changing gear and warning a child at the same time – none of these images would be complete without the fag clamped in the mouth for a minute or seven. There's no point with the e-cigarette. It could just be put down and picked up again. It's not the same.

• **Flicking a fag.** On your coffee break, hovering outside the office on a busy street? Time to go back to work? Throw the dregs of your coffee out of the cup and flick your fag with your middle finger. Watch it sail in a pleasing arc across the pavement, where it will send a shower of sparks into the path of an unsuspecting pleb. You can't flick a vape. It's too expensive. Though you should.

• **Rolling a cigarette** for a part-time smoker who might even be a stranger. The following conversation never takes place between vapers.

'Any smokes?'

'Just rollies . . .'

The part-timer considers his options and whether he can actually roll one.

'Yeah, go on so.'

There's a pause as he makes a pure hames of it.

'Do you want me to roll it for you?'

'Yeah, would you mind?'

'Do you want to lick it yourself?'

'Ah no, you're the expert.'

And suddenly you're setting fire to another person's saliva. You'll never achieve that intimacy with your plastic pipe.

• **Sharing one cigarette among fifteen teenagers.** Teenagers apparently are starting off on vaping *without ever smoking*. Leaving aside the fact that teenagers are unfathomable and don't give a damn what you think anyway, if they are starting off on vaping they are engaging in the most pointless act of teenage rebellion ever. You can't pretend-smoke as an act of rebellion. That would be like telling your parents you're quitting school to join a band to play air guitar.

Chugging Along

They haven't gone away, you know. It's a bright summer's day and you're innocently sauntering down the street, a coy smile playing about your lips to suggest your life is *awesome* (Bx alert). That's when they pounce. They'll catch your eye, an expression of artificially induced cheeriness frozen on their faces, clipboards swinging gaily in their arms, identical coloured windcheaters rustling. If you're a man, they'll call out to you, 'Hey, man', even though you have not expressly given permission for this level of familiarity. (Unless you're in Galway; simply *being* in Galway confers the right on people to call you 'man'.) Although some charities have promised to decommission the clipboard from Irish charity politics, on the street at least, it is still a case of Chugger Law.

Sometimes you will see them assemble before going out to work. Chugger lairs are located on backstreets. It's not clear what goes on in a chuggers' base. One could easily imagine hour-long confidence sessions where they are fed pain au chocolats laced with Prozac and taught how to walk towards a member of the public in a dancy way, waving their arms and shouting, 'Do you have a moment?' Their leader might be a charismatic demagogue, leading his or her charges in a call-and-response chant:

Leader: 'Where does charity begin?'

Chuggers: 'CHARITY BEGINS AT THE DIRECT DEBIT!'

Leader: 'Who has the direct debit?'

Chuggers: 'OULD WANS AND PEOPLE WHO ARE JUST HAPPY TO TALK!'

The seemingly impenetrable confidence of these people is to be grudgingly admired. They are the answer to the question: 'What happens to all the Billie Barry kids once they grow up?'

It's no wonder the industry attracts them. A recent job advertisement for 'street teams' for a particular charity said they were looking for people with a 'genuine desire to overachieve'. It's not clear why they specified 'genuine desire'. Perhaps they had been stung by people pretending to overachieve in the past. Another job spec promises the opportunity to work alongside 'some of the coolest people around'. By 'cool', they mean the kind of people who run through a festival in a mobile-phone commercial, adopting various wacky poses for selfies before getting all thoughtful at sunset.

Elsewhere, a job description promises that most commonplace of workplaces: the dynamic working environment. Because there's nothing worse than a static environment where you just sit at your desk and reply to emails. Chugging is undoubtedly more dynamic but the greatest dynamism is displayed by citizens trying to avoid the Benetton-ad luvvies. Here are the most common legal methods of chugger evasion, so you can walk past them unscathed, much like a gnu might pad softly past a couple of watchful lions:

Eyes to the ground, hands in your pockets and simply drive on through.

Answer your phone. In the absence of a ringtone, authenticity can be achieved by imitating a vibrating sound. Just make sure you're not in a notorious blackspot for coverage.

Suddenly make a ninety-degree turn into the nearest shop. This should be done with caution, as you may end up in a sex shop or, worse, a charity shop where you feel obliged to make a purchase which cancels out your evasive technique.

Start shouting very loudly. While this will usually discourage the chuggers, it may give you an unjust reputation as A Bit Of A Character.

As it turns out, they aren't the worst type of bolloxology going on in some charities, so they get a pass. Chuggers are fairly transparent about what they're up to. You'll never find out a chugger had an overpaid directorship, charged an expenses-paid trip or had no accounts whatsoever even as they were milking the public for cash. Compared to some, chuggers are Mother Teresa. Actually, not Mother Teresa because it turns out that . . . Ah lookit, just give what you can to whomever you trust.

Beard Necessities

It's time to come clean. After embarking on a crusade against bolloxology, it turns out I am chin-deep in it.

'In perhaps his most/only personal work yet, the author opens up about the heart-breaking reality of wearing a beard in a cruel world.'

The abusive epithets are endless. Hipster. Beardy bollix. Yer Man With The Beard. Actually, that's probably it. The beard has made a comeback over the last decade and the reception has been mixed. Each year the death of this phase of the beard is predicted but there are still plenty of men with extensions on their faces. First World War trench lice got rid of the kind of beards associated with explorers dying of typhus in the swamps of the Congo. The beards of the hippies petered out during the punk era. But what will get rid of the current barber-ism?

Beards may be on the way out because they have made the ultimate leap – to mortgage ads. Every billboard that features a young couple, embarking on a consensual relationship with their bank, will now feature a man with a beard. Now that a beard has been associated with a mortgage, it might as well be an elasticated waist and a maroon polo shirt.

It's not easy being a beard-wearer. No man truly knows what his follicles can do until he stops shaving. Many's the man who has found himself let down and tried to hide it with 'styling'. Most beard-wearers don't deserve one, having neither fought the Kaiser nor found King Solomon's mines. Most of us talk too much. Proper bearddom should be reserved for the strong silent type, the Tom Creans of this world, standing on the prow of the *Endurance*, looking out across the South Atlantic Ocean and occasionally philosophizing about how this area was a 'hoor for the pack-ice'.

Or a backwoodsman walking stoically through the forests of the nineteenth-century American frontier, limiting his opinions to pithy observations that this area was a 'divil's own place for the pumas' – the kind of man commemorated by Grizzly Adams, played by actor Dan Haggerty, one of the finest beard-wearers this side of the Cheyenne Trail.

Now beard-wearers are no longer silent. They do a lot of talking about how 'the sound is so much richer on vinyl' and 'their earlier stuff was much better'.

Given the hostile environment for the beard, some precautions should be taken to reduce their potential for bolloxology:

• Avoid putting anything in it, such as knitting, ornaments or reminders.

• Don't shave the bit between your beard and your hair. Your beard is an absence of shaving. Shaving around it makes it look as if you are trying to emphasize your beard. The beard should speak for itself. In fact, if you don't trim around your mouth, it can look like the beard is actually speaking for itself.

• Don't shave any designs into your beard. You are working against nature.

• Avoid describing yourself online as 'a creative'. Creative is an adjective. When you use it as a noun *and* have a beard, you are just making life difficult for the rest of us.

For non-beard-wearers, here are some snap judgements – the most fun kind – to make about the different beards you see.

'To be honest, man, thinking of packing it in. Digital marketing's not my thing. The bird is from Tallinn, so I reckon we'll go there for a while.'

'I'll check, but I think we're out of low-fat. We should be getting more in on Thursday.'

'Did you try switching it off and on again?'

'Well, I have the boat, like, below in Shkibb and a few acres out the road to grow the veg for th'oul organic shop, like. And then there's the band but I shuppose the main business would be the web shtuff.'

'The people of Roscommon/Leitrim will not stand for this.'

3

Standing on Ceremony

Wedded to the Notions

Weddings are a hive of bolloxology. It was ever thus. But whereas before, the Bx might have been simply about throwing money at the event, now there's a lot of 'meaning' and a big emphasis on creating an 'experience'. And if at all possible, there's the hope that it might go viral.

There are still people who get married just for the intrinsic experience of it and, at worst, the reactions of those who are there. But increasingly it's also about the people who aren't there – friends and strangers – and what those people think of it when they see it on their phones.

In theory, the deregulation of the wedding industry has been an important step in the modernization of the country. Finally, people could have it all their own way and get married somewhere that was special to them and not feel compelled to use a church. But as thousands of years of Eastern philosophy will tell you, having it all your own way is a recipe for a different type of discontent. There is an arms race now in trying to make the wedding 'memorable'.

Don't forget, though, your wedding will always be memorable to you yourself, even if you hold it in a registry office that is temporarily housed in a prefab behind a Spar. On the other hand, even if you arrive on an elephant mahouted by Lady Gaga, there will still be guests in years to come who won't be able to remember whose wedding that was because they were aged 26–32 at the time and it was the eighth wedding they were at *that year*.

Wedding bolloxology has taken off in a number of ways:

> • For many couples, the entrance sets the tone for the day. You can't just walk up the red carpet at the Dungouvney Castle Arms. It has to be a statement. The reality is that you splurge fifteen grand on a James Bond/Cadbury's Milk Tray/ Bourne series-themed video but the videographer can't get rid of any footage and makes it twenty minutes long so that it stops being funny about two minutes in. It's too long to go viral and, by the guests' reaction, they have swiftly moved on to discussing other matters such as 'Who's the guest who's already drinking the one that's one too many?' and 'Is there any sign of the first wife?' So much so that the couple's actual physical entrance goes unnoticed.

• The vows have become mini-epics in themselves, often reflecting the shared interests of the couple. So you might have them written in Old English, or played out as a *Game of Thrones* scene, or an All-Ireland winning speech. (God help them if their favourite programme is *EastEnders*.) The vows themselves might be written on rice paper which is set on fire and released in a Chinese lantern (not advisable if the ceremony is held indoors).

• The first dance has lost all control. It used to be an opportunity for the entire guestlist to gawk at the couple as they danced awkwardly through a song that they NEVER REALIZED WAS THIS LONG. But love and awkwardness with all the neighbours watching is what married life is all about. Nowadays, it has become a showcase for the collective talents of a segment of the guests – Riverdancing, hakaing. This is all great for the people involved but many of the guests will get the 'oh great, there's a guy at the house party with a guitar' feeling.

• The cake has lost all sense of proportion – sometimes literally. Nowadays you're nobody unless your cake is ultra-Instagrammable. If you can't get Mary Berry to bake it for you, then your best bet is to go with a 'statement' – shape it like a globe to represent all the places you've visited together, with flavours to match. Or individual cupcakes for every guest in the shape of their own heads.

- 'Afters' food has experienced runaway inflation. The crushed ham sandwich has morphed into a full midnight feast, which is almost as filling as the dinner itself. In fact, strategic guests could, in theory, decline the invitation, get a day's work done and then turn up for a late-night banquet and save €75–100 on the present.

Church grounds

'Would you not just go with the church anyway? Ah do. Nana'd have a fit.'

The church wedding has a number of advantages that you may not be aware of.

Practice
The church wedding is a great preparation for married life. Choosing a location for the ceremony so as not to show your mother up in front of Her Side is an example of the kind of compromise you'll be making in future, and compromise is essential to a happy marriage.

Concentration
Civil ceremonies are all full of 'meaning'. You have to concentrate on everything in case you miss something. 'The bride and groom will now do the Lotto as a symbol of the luck they hope to have in their marriage' or 'The

bride and groom will now kill a bullock as a symbol of plenty in their marriage.' Blink and you might find you are the only person not showering the happy couple with M&Ms.

It was easier during the mass. You could sit down and look around to see who came from the Other Side of the family.

Dramatic tension

Have you ever been at the perfect wedding? The weather was beautiful. The celebrant was understanding and wise – shur, wasn't she happily married herself for twenty years? The ceremony was laden with symbolism pertinent to the couple. And yet afterwards you felt something was missing. Oh, it was a *lovely* wedding but it needed *something* . . .

It needed dramatic tension. Having a church wedding adds all sorts of unknowns to the affair. A priest is a wild card on a wedding day. He can't be controlled by the bride and groom. Will he do the shake hands or not? His sermon is the best man's speech backed by doctrine. He might even be one of those priests who has long-held aspirations to be a recording artist in Nashville. Being an 'old friend of the family' is no guarantee of predictability. He is, after all, an old friend of *one side* of the family. Is he a cranky priest? What happens if he rips into the material world and the wedding party with its fleet of Mercedes outside?

But even without that, there are the explosions of

laughter if the priest cracks a joke. IMAGINE a priest cracking a joke in a church!

There is a slight chance he may go on about traditional roles within a marriage, telling the bride not to be afraid to stay at home and look after the children, despite the pressures of the modern world. Obviously this is more entertaining for the guests than for the bride and groom but weddings are about the guests. Otherwise why would they invite us?

A change of scenery

The church-reception divide meant a chance for debriefing. You got into the car and gossiped. 'Who was yer wan in the green? Did she think this was the Playboy mansion or what? What did you make of the priest, hah? Ah, the page boy – the dote!'

That bit was over. A line drawn under it. God had signed off on the thing. Now it was time for vol-au-vents.

If both the wedding and the reception are all in the one place, it can be a bit claustrophobic. You finish the ceremony and then . . . where do you go? Dinner isn't for three hours. If you're Someone's Cousin (see page 60) you can probably drink right through and become the ledgebag with his tie around his head for Journey's 'Don't Stop Believing' but not everyone can manage that. Either way, you might be stuck with the same people for up to twelve hours. You don't even spend that much time with your spouse.

Going to hell

If there is a heaven and hell, it goes without saying you've a better chance of avoiding eternal damnation if you've picked up a bit of paperwork and a few sacraments along the way. Would it *hurt* to take a few precautions, just to be on the safe side? Surely there's no harm in having a church wedding, even if you mumble the responses and hope to God (funnily enough) that they're not the ones that were gotten rid of when the New Mass came in?

In a similar way, a 'naming ceremony' for a child will be meaningful and all that, but the child being tapped gently with a hazel rod to represent being welcomed into the bosom of Gaia just isn't going to cut it if the Divil himself is at the crossroads, looking for souls. Just get straight to the bit where you are asked to reject Satan and all his works and empty promises. Plus, there is always the possibility of a child doing a deliciously timed fart at the rejection of the Lord of Evil.

Pre-pre-marriage course

Whatever the reason, if you are going to have a wedding ceremony in a church, you can't just turn up at the match and expect to tog-off. You'll have to go to training. The two main stages are going on 'one of these pre-marriage yokes', and meeting the priest.

During the first hour of a pre-marriage course, couples may be tense, expecting a priest to come in any second and tell them about married life but no priest would bother with that now. He might turn up later on with some forms. Mainly, pre-marriage courses have a bit of gentle questioning and role play about potential situations couples might encounter in their married life. It's gentle in case it accidentally reveals partners to be completely incompatible.

Ideally, one role play they should consider bringing in would be How To Go Up To The Priest After Mass To Ask About The Church.

Firstly, wait until the priest is finished his conversations with the local stalwarts – the type who know exactly what to say in the way of a light-hearted to-and-fro exchange with a priest:

> 'Your own club got a bad going over at the weekend, Father.'
>
> 'Oh, stop. Ah, but the referee was a disgrace.'
>
> 'You'll have to forgive still though, Father.'
>
> 'I hope he doesn't come in to me for confession, anyway. Hah?'

Or they might have a bit of church business to discuss:

> 'Listen, Father, would you include my sister-in-law Connie in your intentions next week? It'll be her anniversary.'
>
> 'No bother at all, Mrs Donegan. How long is it now?'

'Four years, Father.'

'Four years? I suppose it is. She'll be well settled-in Above anyway. There was only one place she was going. Poor Connie.'

'I know, Father. Thanks, Father.'

Secondly, he knows you know he knows. Priests know the way with church weddings. You haven't 'been' in ages and you mightn't go afterwards. This won't be an audit of your soul. But you need to make some small talk. Priests like talking to young people because they don't talk so much about their ailments or who they're not speaking to.

'Hello, Father.'

'Hello, eh . . .'

'Kelly Sheehan, Father.'

'OH, KELLY. HOW ARE YOU AT ALL?! I don't know when I saw you last. And Steven, is it? An Offaly man, I hear. Ah well, no one's perfect, hahaha!'

'No, Father.'

'And how's your mam?'

'Oh, she's great.'

'Still doing the walking – I see her every day up and down the road with Sharon. A great woman for the walking.'

'She calls it her therapy.'

'Therapy is right, haha. We could all do with that. And Dad is well?'

'He is, Father.'

'And tell me, how is her mother?'

'Nana is flying, Father. Picking out hats.'

'Picking out h— Haha, congratulations then, I suppose. And I suppose I should congratulate you as well, Steven. It is you, is it, haha?'

There are certain handy phrases to say to priests . . .

'This boy is very quiet. I suppose he can't get a word in with you, Kelly, haha, is that it?'

'That's right, Father. I have him well trained.'

Eventually you'll get to the religion bit . . .

'Right so. Ye're getting married. And what date were ye looking at?'

'August, Father.'

'August – wait till I get the book out now. August is busy. A popular time of year. And you're a Catholic, are you, Steven?'

'Um . . . yeah. I wouldn't be that much of a mass-goer now, Father . . .'

'Yerra, shure neither am I.'

'Eh . . . Sorry?'

'Haha! I'm only codding you!'

'Oh, right. Very good, Father, haha.'

'Shur, lookit, very few are but the main thing is that you were baptized anyway.'

'Oh, I was, yeah.'

'That just makes it easier. Of course, it takes all kinds nowadays. I had a couple in the other day. She was . . . waittillseenow, she was from Thailand and he was a Brazilian. And he was a Catholic but she was "of the Buddhist persuasion".'

It doesn't 'got to be perfect'

Regardless of where the ceremony takes place, it's no harm to have a few checks and balances because married life just isn't perfect and one shouldn't feel pressurized to have the Perfect Day.

One correction to perfection can be provided by The Fathers' speeches. It is sometimes hard to know how long an Irish ould lad will go on for. This may be the only time they will speak publicly in their lives. The quietest of men have produced Churchillian masterpieces, surprising everyone with quotes from Ovid, while the blowiest of golf-club president blowhards have unfortunately done exactly what was expected of them and gone on for forty minutes. It does, however, take the sting out of the perfect day which preceded it, thus allowing the other couples who had a normal wedding to feel a bit better about themselves.

And then there's Someone's Cousin. This guest may not even be an actual cousin. It's unclear to all the other guests what his connection is to the couple but everyone will remember him and assume that maybe he is . . . well . . . someone's cousin. Here's how to spot him:

• Tie loosened, smoking a fag outside the church.

• Despite the meticulous itinerary-planning of the bride and groom, he *somehow* manages to find a pub in between the ceremony and the meal and waylays a group of guests who therefore arrive late to the reception venue, spoiling the choreographed entrance of the bride and groom, who were supposed to twerk their way down a slide from the balcony over the dance floor.

• As the long day draws to a close, some guests will make their excuses. The music will be too much for aunties and nans. But Someone's Cousin will be in his element doing Mad Bastard dancing, knocking over a page boy, roaring at the band to stop playing that hippy-dippy stuff and throw on some AC/DC.

• He takes it upon himself to represent the Local Chapter Of The Union Of Disenfranchised Wedding

Guests Who Want To Go Into The Residents Bar But Are Not Residents. Those negotiations go as follows:

Someone's Cousin: 'Holdzonasecondnow, wass yername?'

Patient Annoyed Bar Manager: 'Pavel.'

Someone's Cousin *[arm around Pavel's shoulder]*: 'Pavel, whereufromPavel?'

Pavel: 'I am from Czech Republic.'

[There follows a long diversion about Someone's Cousin being in Prague once.]

Someone's Cousin: 'Pavel, listentomenowmygoodman, we jzust want wan dzhrink to celebratezhappy couple.'

At this point, one aunt may turn racist.

Census Sensibility

Church sacraments are a real 'come to God' (or not come to God as the case may be) moment in the dialogue between the generations. Most of the time, discussions about religion are avoided. The cohort of the population who haven't really admitted to their mothers that they've stopped going to mass can, by and large, get away without discussing it. Apart from the wedding, no one need say nothing to no one about nothing. And then, every five years, a form blunders through the door asking the question out loud like a big eejit.

Every five years, the Republic of Ireland takes a census of the population. There are some secondary purposes, such as planning the future needs of the nation, but the main questions that need to be asked are:

- How many people's mothers – and sometimes fathers – fill out the form, putting them down as Catholic whether they like it or not?

- How many people's mothers and fathers fill out the form and would be 'OK' with the children choosing to put down whatever religion they wanted but don't want to upset *His Mother* who's living with them?

- How many people go on social media urging people to put down 'No Religion' based on definite criteria of what constitutes having a religion?

- How many people go on social media feeling 'oppressed' by other people telling them what to put down as their religion?

- How many people go on social media feeling 'oppressed' by other people complaining about them telling people what to put down as their religion?

• How many people really just don't want to get into this because they're spending too much time online anyway?

The thing is, religion is hard to quantify on a checkbox.

It is said that in any given population, approximately one-third are devout, one-third are non-believers and one-third are *sorta, kinda, ah shur, I suppose, you know, didn't really think about it.*

In the past in Ireland, nearly everyone went to mass if they knew what was good for them. The one-third wisha-I-don't-knows stayed at the back, chatting, smoking and heading off before communion to beat the rush and get the *Sunday World*, and the one-third non-believers contemplated writing a novel about the dark heart of the hypocritical Irish countryside until they saw what happened to your man whose book was banned.

While some people, who haven't been to mass since Ronnie Whelan scored against the Russians, just plain lied about their religion on the most recent census, there must surely be a few who hedged their bets. There may be no connection between getting the children baptized and waiting lists for schools – just a sort of gut feeling that, with the Health Service the way it is, and the pensions time-bomb ticking, it mightn't be any harm to leave a few doors open for one's older years.

The Irish have always been an equivocating race. We say things like 'Well, you didn't hear this from me, now' and ''Tis you said it', so it's no surprise some of us might indulge in box-ticking exercises, just to be on the safe side with the Man Above, if He exists.

Regardless of your religion, the census could still ask some questions that are more pertinent.

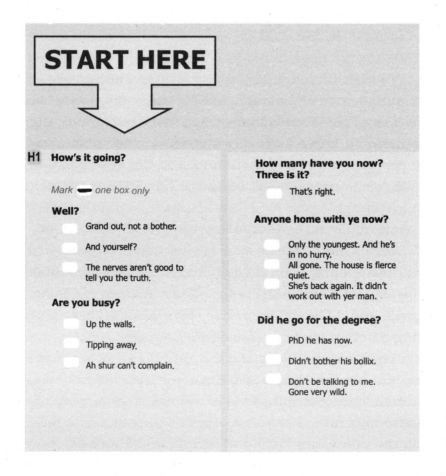

START HERE

H1 **How's it going?**

Mark ⬤ *one box only*

Well?

☐ Grand out, not a bother.

☐ And yourself?

☐ The nerves aren't good to tell you the truth.

Are you busy?

☐ Up the walls.

☐ Tipping away.

☐ Ah shur can't complain.

How many have you now? Three is it?

☐ That's right.

Anyone home with ye now?

☐ Only the youngest. And he's in no hurry.
☐ All gone. The house is fierce quiet.
☐ She's back again. It didn't work out with yer man.

Did he go for the degree?

☐ PhD he has now.

☐ Didn't bother his bollix.

☐ Don't be talking to me. Gone very wild.

4

Getting from A to Bx

Plane and Simple

Maybe it's the altitude. Maybe it's the last vestige of the glory days of aircraft travel when there was no danger of plebs applauding when the plane landed. But something happens to the accents of the cabin crew when they pick up the intercom on an Airbus 330 to talk to the passengers. Then again, maybe they were born with it.

She (and the occasional he) greets you with a friendly 'how's it going?' as she checks your boarding pass (just to make sure you haven't somehow eluded three checkpoints along the way). She's a Rose-of-Tralee-level Grand Girl or like a Favourite Aunt who was all 'not a bother' and 'ah shur, can't complain'.

Then, somewhere along the line, she switches mode in an almost Jekyll-and-Hyde transformation. The accent becomes infused with vowel sounds that are extremely rare. 'For your comfort and safety' becomes all the one word; 'fastened' takes on a life of its own;

and there is a huge emphasis on 'enjooying' the flight. There are recommendations for car hire that no one ever takes up, and a fervent wish that we will see each other in future.

> 'Feyekimfirtnsifty plis ensiur yur seatbalts r s'curely faaahrstened, yur ahmrasts daine, yur traytable stoored and your seatbaacks intheflea pright p'sition. Any caowts or baags mizbee stooored underdseatinfrontoffyiu or in d'ooverhad lawkers.'

Perhaps it's a bit harsh to call this bolloxology. In fact, it's a bit harsh to criticize anything that happens 33,000 feet in the air when you're the passenger and these people are looking after you. Maybe it's just a small case of antique notions.

Pilots, on the other hand, don't feel the need to modulate their voices. All male pilots sound like Dick Moran from *Glenroe* – smooth, like a good whiskey. They may tell you about what they've been up to, as though they're trying to seduce you in a hotel bar in Hong Kong. They don't even mention safety procedures. They're flying the damn plane. They ARE the safety procedure.

We don't deserve them, really. We still *are* the kind of people who applaud on landing.

IRELAND'S NEW TOURIST ZONES

GAME OF THRONES
FILMING LOCATIONS

GAME OF
SCONES
TEA SHOP

WILDEST
ATLANTIC
WAY

Great
view
of America.

Ireland's
Historic
FUEL LAUNDERING
Border

WILDER
ATLANTIC
WAY

THE
"We got
a deal"
HOTEL
HOTSPOT

Ireland's
Bypassed
Middle

THE
BIG
SCHMOKE

WILD
ATLANTIC
WAY

INTENSE
"ARE WE
THERE
YET?"
ZONE.

THE INDIFFERENT IRISH SEA MEANDER

The dawn pint

The dawn pint is a tiny bit of self-determination and freedom that is also Bx. It's a time-honoured tradition of Irish and UK airports since our ancestors – OK, your uncle – first realized that airports are a sort of Big Rock Candy Mountain where normal pub hours don't apply.

There are three types of dawn drinker:

• **The group of young lads with One Mad Bastard at its heart**. OMB may have been out the night before, will be a liability for the rest of the holiday, probably is an actual alcoholic (but not in the Irish sense), and is on a twenty-year quest to avoid the gaping hole in his life. But for now he's a good man to get the party started in the airport. The gang of lads will be arranged in concentric circles around OMB in decreasing magnitude of OMBness.

• **The group of ould lads off to a match or a bit of golf.** Arms folded across blue TQJs (Table Quiz Jumpers), they eschew the lurid-coloured drinks of the youth and rest a pint on their bellies. They will spend the holiday speculating on how the only thing stopping Yer Wan Over There throwing herself at them was the ring on their finger.

• **The uneasy man and his tight-lipped wife.** This is a man not normally given to dawn drinking but since this flight was booked he's been looking forward to ordering a pint and sending a picture of that pint to his daughter at work with the caption 'On our holidays' while his wife sends her details of the hotel, the burglar alarm code (again) and warnings about things that need to be switched off and unplugged. She has pursed her lips in advance of this moment.

'And shur, you can have a white wine.'

'I don't want a white wine. Declan, it's half-FIVE in the morning.'

'But we're on our holidays. Look, I'll get you a white wine.'

'I won't drink it.'

[Some time later]

'This is the job, isn't it? Sit in there for a photo with your wine till I send it to Sarah. You haven't touched your wine.'

'I told you I didn't want it. How can you even enjoy it at this hour? You'll be dying for the lav on the plane now and complaining about there being no room in there. Couldn't you have waited until we got to the hotel? And Sarah'll probably have that photo put up onto her Facebook and they'll all think you're an alcoholic.'

You'll never see this kind of ceremony before any flight to America. You don't want to go through Preclearance Immigration without the full command of your faculties in case you say something stupid that would have thirteen of them sitting on you and you'd never get to Disneyland again.

Immigration clearance is a bolloxology- and notions-free zone. Even the typeface, which has been all Arial and Helvetica and welcoming everywhere else in the airport, becomes official and serifed and stern. The officials – unless you get the one who's a bit of fun – won't take any of your small talk. They're watching you to see whether you're just a normal eejit or a terrorist who's made careful study of Irish eejitry.

How do these people get on when they're off duty and exposed to the half-talk and relentless messing of Irish discourse? Do they need to stay away from us lest we compromise their mission?

They are just doing their job or, as we call it, zero craic. As if the world's terrorists can be defeated by A Lad Who's Sound.

Taxi Driver

We take Irish taxi drivers for granted. It's only when you travel to another country and your taxi driver says nothing except sigh at the paucity of the tip you've just given him, that you realize how much value you get at home: at least twenty minutes of ye both talking bollox.

A conversation with an Irish taxi driver – particularly a Dublin taxi driver – is like one of those old Choose Your Own Adventure books that used to be around before the internet. How the journey goes can be influenced by you. The taxi driver will leave an ellipsis at the end of every sentence and, depending on how you respond, any one of a number of predefined paths can be chosen:

Example 1
The driver alludes to the presence of some new housing estates. This is a clue that he would like to talk about the state of the country following the building boom of the Celtic Tiger.

>If you a) ignore the bait, go to page 34*.
>If you choose b) and say, 'I know what you mean', go to page 100.
>Or do you c) reply factually but with a leading statement.

*Legal disclaimer: This is a hypothetical page 34. Any resemblance to page 34 of this book is wholly coincidental. Readers are advised to go to page 34 only at their own risk. Bolloxology, Inc. is not responsible for any 'emotional distress and loss of earnings' you may suffer as a result of this.

Note on legal disclaimer: We include this just to be on the safe side as you wouldn't know who'd try to sue. We'd have devoted a whole bolloxology section to some people's tendency to drink ten pints down the pub, fall over and, instead of taking responsibility for their own actions, take the pub to court and get fifty grand, but we'd be afraid someone would take offence and 'do us for defamation'.

You choose c)

'Actually, we've a few of the new estates around the corner. They're half-empty still. Think they're in NAMA.'

'I was going to ask you that, actually. Still empty? Suffern jaysus. A disaster it was, that place. And that fella a course – he's off in Dubai now sellin' sand to the Arabs, I suppose.'

'I didn't hear.'

'He IS. Because I had his daughter in the cab a couple of years ago. Well, ye wanna see the state of her. After a night out. One of them posh places on Dawson Street, it was. And this lad in with her – her boyfriend or whatever. Pure bogey he was. On the sniff of course he was, so actin' the bollix. Says he's a DJ and he's givin' it "all that" to me, mixin' records with his hands or I don't know what the f*ck. And she's on the phone *screamin'* at the father that he hasn't sent the f*ckin' money through and she's threatenin' to set Revenue on him, sayin' she'll tell them he's in the Gulf livin' it up. AND THEN, when we get to where they're goin', the boyfriend's arguing with me over the fare. And she's givin' me, "Do you know who my father is?" an all that. And I said, "I know who he was but he's a f*ckin' nobody now." Well, that shut her up. They get out an anyways and she spits at the window. I'm tellin' ye, these rich f*ckers are the real

72

scumbags. Give me a junkie any day. At least he'd
be ourrovih, the poor bastard.'

Example 2

Your final destination does not provide a sufficient
springboard for conversation. Do you:

a) Leave it at that.
b) Use your departure city as an example of where
they know how to run a country, not like here.

You choose b)

'Where were ye flyin' from?'

[You mention your departure city.]

'It's lovely there, isn't it? I've heard.'

'Spotless too. Not a bit of litter around or anything.
And SAFE.' *[Then drop it in like a grenade, after a
one-second delay.]* 'Not like here.'

'Ah Jaysus, who are ya tellin'? I was up around
Mountjoy Square the other morning. About five
o'clock. Dropping this fella off. And I parked up there.
Just got a coffee and a f*ckin' donut or something
from the twenty-four-hour place there – you know.
Just drinkin' me coffee and I looked over and there
was this black fella – cool as you like, not a f*ckin'
bother on him. Dumpin' a mattress at the wall.'

'Did you say anything to him?'

'NO, I did in me bollix – none of my business what he does.'

The driver has mentioned a black fella.

For tacit acceptance or noncommittal silence, choose a) A weakly muttered 'Imagine that' and proceed to *'And Don't Get Me Started On The Chinese Cyclists'*.
For an uncomfortable taxi journey, choose b) 'Well, I don't see what the colour of his skin has to do with it.'
In for a penny, in for a pound, choose c) 'As for the Romanians ...' At which point the taxi driver criticizes *you* for being a bit racist as his brother is actually married to a Romanian.
As a diplomatic compromise, choose d) 'Shur, the Irish are just as bad.'

The Cycle of Life

Cycling has changed. It used to just be a way of getting around the place because there weren't any other options. Everyone had a bike so no one stole them. You'd often find a pile of Raleigh Triumphs leaning against a hedge as the children who owned them got up to some sort of rural mischief in an orchard. Or two hundred black cast-iron 'cycling machines' propped up against the wall of a church while a priest inside told the congregation to be careful about cycling as it could give rise to impure thoughts. Now everything is different. Cycling is a choice. And like a lot of choices, people have put a lot of thought into it. Here are some of the more self-aware cyclotypes.

Whimsy McQuirk

Ms McQuirk cycles a bike decorated with stencils of butterflies, with white tyres and a front basket made of woven barley. The basket contains some notepaper on which is written the lyrics of a bittersweet song about two strangers who meet and fall in love in a park over the course of an afternoon but never find out one another's names. McQuirk's clothes are 'boho' in style, many of them salvaged from jumble sales (to which all attendees will cycle on similar bikes). McQuirk struggles with the privations which modern life forces upon her. The disgustingly modern, expanded polyurethane foam in a bicycle helmet is an affront to her sensibilities but cranial experts assured her that her original one – made of distressed walnut – was impractical.

Conchudhbhairdh Curator

Whimsy McQuirk may be accompanied by her life partner Conchudhbhairdh Curator – a man who looks like an Edwardian carpenter but was born in Monasterevin. He will be riding a large black bike that looks like it was once used to deliver a telegram announcing the outbreak of war against the Boers but was actually bought in a Cycle-to-Work-Tax-Rebate shop, having been imported from China where they heard we're mad into this kind of thing.

Family bike

Once Whimsy and Conchudhbhairdh have children, all distressed walnut helmets and fixed-gear messenger bikes are sold or abandoned. Safety is the watchword now and children are wrapped in Styrofoam as the family makes its way along the road, the parents ulcerating themselves with tension at each passing hazard.

Courier-ous

Some people are really fast and daring on bicycles and, boy, do they want you to know it. They ride machines whose frames are so thin and light their very existence is a matter of conjecture. They're the ones who can stay upright at traffic lights – if they ever obey them – without resting either foot on the ground. They may also be wearing a head-cam to record incidents with other road users, which they upload to YouTube but only end up making themselves look silly.

Now-I'm-not-a-racer-but

Travelling at the same speed as Courier-ous, the NINARB is a different animal. He (it's always a he) passes you effortlessly while you are out of the saddle, puffing away. His calf muscles look like cantaloupes being smuggled underneath his skin. However, there is nothing cool about NINARBs – perhaps because they wear outfits so tight, their genitals have to be detached and sent ahead of them (usually via cycle courier).

They are also to be found on Sundays in large groups training for the CYCLE TO HELL, GET SLAPPED AROUND THE PLACE BY HAIRY DEMONS AND THEN THE JOURNEY BACK FROM HELL endurance race.

Chief among this group is The Man Who Looked At The Scales Or Who Got A Bit Of A Health Scare And Said That's It. Aged forty-plus, with a bike that cost more than the line of cars he is holding up, he is getting out of the house, away from the bewildering teenagers hunched over glowing screens, cyberbullying each other. Out on the open road, his mind is free at last.

Ninety per cent of his social media photos consist of him standing behind the bike on the side of a mountain in the rain with the slogan 'Looking forward to the pints later!!'

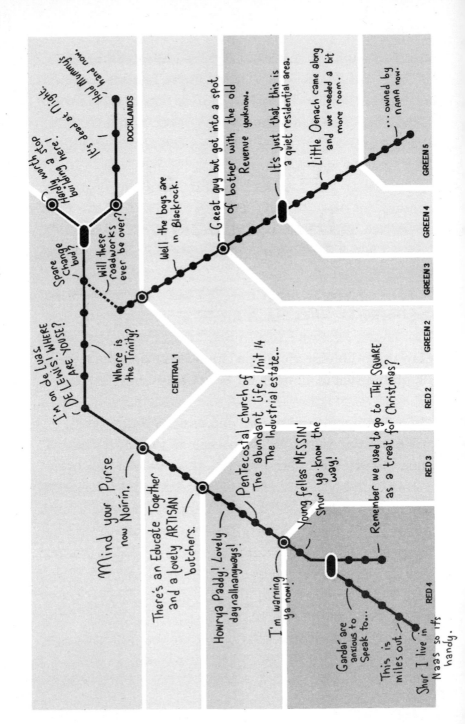

5

Humans of Bolloxology

Spoken Word Poetry

Hermione Mulligan is a performance poet from Shanstroglish in County Roscommon.

Yeah, I guess my poems are about everything, really. It's not like the stuff we had to learn in school. You know, all that 'figure out the themes of seventeenth-century metaphysical poets', who were clearly in unhealthy co-dependent relationships with God. My poems are all about performance. Like, um, I guess there are no rules to spoken word. It's about whatever you know, you feel and um. I remember, like, I was at the Galvanized Shed and Cans Festival down, I think it was in Carlow? It's a pretty new festival so it was just so, like, we went in over a ditch? And that was my first gig. It was raining so the tent was pretty full. But I just, like, winged it? And I guess that the formula I basically sort of stumbled on was that:

• *The last word of each line should be said at the start of the next line. I'd heard a load of other poets and they all seem to leave their words hanging. It sounded really cool.*

• *Sometimes I say a load of words that sound roughly the same even if they've nothing to do with the theme. Then I'll repeat a couple of lines and also shout a bit in the middle. This is always a good one for audience members for whom this is their first poetry-slam. They'll expect a bit of 'alternative'. Here's an example:*

Carrots

Indecision incision into my skin MY

SKIN. From the earth cries a

Beetle. Beetle Church Steeple Sheet

Metal welded by my

Dreams you may say this is boll

Oxology but oxen drag the weight of my

Thoughts. Through the gate of the

FACTORY. IN WHICH THEY TOIL TO MAKE THE

TOGS. THE TOGS THAT hold the

Legs that KICK THE

POINTS. We are told to take the

Points and the goals will come but who is the

Goalkeeper?

This next one's called 'Biscuits'. It's about how we are all really just tools of the Biscuit Establishment.

Biscuits
Custard creams their
Screams echoing inside my mind my body as
I rip off the top and then
Lick the cream and then finish
With the bottom bit NOOOOO
The government shouts pouts, gets a new
Rig-out for the wedding of church and state. Don't be
Messing with them biscuits. They say sagely, what age are you
Seven? Just eat them properly. Just
BITE THEM BITE THEM You
Are the same with the Twirls but
I SAY TO
THEM THIS IS NOT YOUR CHOICE ABOUT
HOW I EAT MY BISCUIT OR DIP MY TWIRL IN AND
OUT OF
THE TEA. I ASSERT MY PROPER
TEA AND MY RIGHT TO EAT IT PEACEFULLY
WITHOUT INTERFERENCE FROM
THE PATRIARCHY BECAUSE WHO ARE YOU THAT
SHOUT AND
FUSS TO SAY HOW WE MUSTN'T AND
MUST EAT OUR CONFECTIONERY AND LIVE
WHILE YOUR LAWS AGAINST MY PEOPLE AND
NATURE AND LOVE AND LEARNING AND BURNING
AND YEARNING AND BERTIE AHERNING JUST
Take the biscuit.

Reconstruction Industry Worker

Billy Dooley is a former builder who has diversified and found regular work in Ireland's history industry. The sector has undergone a 500 per cent growth since 2012 but it is expected that revenues will fall off a cliff in 2022.

I was supposed to go to Australia there with the biys but I kinda got homesick before I left, when they all came to the party for me going away. There was no work here for a while but then, when the commemorations came along, the whole reconstruction industry picked up. I got a bit of work in 2013 on the Lockout stuff and then a bit of gunrunning and a bit of Battle of Clontarf stuff in 2014. Then it was quiet for a while, but recently it's picked up nicely. This year I've been rushed off me feet. I'd say there wasn't a week went by when I wasn't wearing heavy brown trousers and a flat cap and running around with a wooden gun. I'm hoping now to be busy till 2022 and then shur, it'll be time to commemorate something else. Maybe I'll be a guard who brings women to Magdalene laundries and runaway children back to industrial schools.

They like me because I'll do the work a lot of lads wouldn't. I don't mind being a strike breaker or a shnakey Viking or a spy. This year now I've mainly been RIC lads shot in the back in some half-arsed offshoot of the Rising but the big one is 2019. I'd say I'll be non-stop Black and Tan or British Army spy for a couple of years.

And then I'll try and get the gig to shoot Michael Collins.

The Next Great Irish Novelist

Oisín Ó Foghlú is an author. With three unpublished novels about the dark side of Irish rural life, he is anxious to make his mark in the literary world.

I've always been attracted to the dark side of the human character. Especially in rural Ireland where there is a huge darkness and a sadness all the time. It's the rain. It seeps into everything. That's what I try to bring across in my novels. And everyone has dark secrets and usually it turns out they were adopted or abandoned. Or both. Twice. The other big theme for me is how closed-down we are emotionally. I hope we don't lose that. I know the Irish are talking a lot more about themselves. Which is great for our mental health but terrible for the future of the Irish novel because we need people to bottle stuff up. Especially men. Men not saying what they feel is the basis of most of my novels. Not saying a word about what's wrong with them. Here's an excerpt from my first book.

Flanagan looked at the old man. They hardly knew each other any more. He spat into the fire

It was that
Wetting
Kind of Rain

Oisín Ó Foghlú
A Novel

"...a devastating portrayal of a
life of silence, isolation and
amber weather warnings for
precipitation."
New York Times

and lit a cigarette. The old man looked back at him and slurped his tea. He lit a cigarette as well. The blustery rain hammered against the window. Then his father spat into the fire. But missed slightly. The spit hung off the mantelpiece, gloating at them. As if it was saying: Look at the two of ye, unable to talk to each other.

'Why did you do it, Da?' The question hung in the air like the smoke from Flanagan's cigarette. All coily and smoky. The old man was silent. With quivering hands he tapped at his iPhone 6, which seemed incongruous given the overall bleakness of the situation. 'Why did you do it?' Flanagan demanded again.

'What?'

'You know what!'

The old man said nothing and switched on the television. Dr Phil was on.

'You really need to talk to each other,' Dr Phil was saying to a couple.

'TALK!' bellowed the old man. 'WHAT GOOD DID TALK EVER DO?'

Flanagan looked over at him with the kind of disgust you only find in ramshackle farmhouses. What a boor. The man was so closed-down inside. No interest in talking about feelings or what was wrong with him. He once went four days with a shovel stuck in his head. Said he wasn't going to any doctor like one of them gay fellas would. Suddenly, Flanagan missed his mother. Why did she have to go away and die? Or at least he assumed she was dead. He was very young and didn't remember and maybe that might prove significant later on.

Maor Uisce

Packie Geary is a clubman through and through. The star, along with his uncle and nephew, of the Clangrudgeon 2004 Junior D hurling league triumph, he has found a new lease of life elsewhere in a 'related field'.

I spose I got into the maor stuff when I was injured there a few years ago. 'Tis handy enough, like. You'd bring on the water, janaw but the main job is when the whole thing kicks off. A lot of lads now would be fairly sensitive and open about their feelings but I like to keep the whole thing bottled up just so I'm good and ready to lamp a fella when something boils over on the pitch.

The important thing is to know when to go on. You can't go on after a few slaps because you'll be spotted a mile off. You could bring your water with you but it would slow you down, so the main thing is to have your hands free and pile in when the ref has lost complete control. You know the ref has lost control if one of the managers runs on to protect him but is actually throwing in a few digs himself.

You'll get the odd ban, like, but shur, they wouldn't know who you'd be with the hood up, and the club would always say they didn't know who I was and that there were a few break-ins at the clubhouse and some bibs stolen.

A personal low point for me was in '09 in a county semi-final when I was in the toilet during a schmozzle and I missed the whole thing. The club were very good to me, though, and stood beside me and brought me back again after a fortnight.

The Generation Emigration Candidate

Carolyn Fitzgerald-Hourican left Ireland in 2012 after graduating with a degree and all.

I was working in a café but I wasn't getting to use my skills so I needed a break. I needed to get away from Ireland with its closed minds and primitive laws vis-à-vis women. A lot of my friends were going to Utopiastan so I just threw caution to the wind and came out here.

Don't get me wrong. Utopiastan isn't perfect. Obviously, like, you hear stories about suppression of pro-democratic parties and people getting thirty lashes for insulting the president. But my new Utopiastani friends don't mention much about it. Or if they do, I don't really see them afterwards. They're probably too embarrassed about being such downers. And as I look down from my gated compound, I see a generosity of spirit, a vibrant culture.

People here are so non-judgemental, especially if you're white and work in the oil industry. Not like Ireland with its small-mindedness and unwillingness to take a risk.

I'm so glad I took the risk and came out here where everything is looked after. I suppose I was really after some adventure and a life-changing experience that was well-paid and tax-free. The weather here is amazing and we're out doing so much fun stuff. My Nepalese servant laughs and says, 'Oh, Miss Fitzgerald-Hourican, you are always out. You must be as exhausted as I am, haha.'

There is such a sense of national pride out here that we could really learn from in Ireland. Like, if the interests of the ruling elite are threatened, they are just, like, so proactive about fighting wars in other countries by proxy or sending in aircraft to bomb rebel positions.

If I ever do come back to Ireland, once it has fixed its

appalling treatment of women and minorities, I think that's the outlook and the culture I'd like to introduce. That get-up-and-go attitude.

The Angry Columnist

Jim Moore is a columnist who shoots from the hip and takes no prisoners. His forthright views make him always good value for a quote and he is a regular provocative panellist on one of those programmes that solves nothing.

I should explain my job. It's basically to have an opinion every week on the Big Thing That's Happened. Most of the time I don't have any direct experience of it but what I'll do is just take one bit of the experiences I do have, twist it a bit so it fits and then hammer my point home with a mallet. The important thing is to time the contrarian viewpoint correctly so it looks 'bravest' and gets the most 'traction on social media'.

Mostly I'll be sort of curmudgeonly and right wing. I used to be left wing but then I got a bit better paid and I figured out that most of the problem was the poor and the way they bring a lot of it on themselves or are just plain unlucky. Also, the metrics are good on the paper's website when I go a bit hard on one of the PC brigade's pet causes.

Plus, I simply ran out of things to say. There are only so many opinions and, as I got older, I was doing a lot less living and all the people I used to go to dinner parties with were also doing better for themselves so there was only one way to go.

Anyway, must dash. There's been a big typhoon and I need to write something that begins with 'Although the scenes have been distressing, are we really the ones to help . . .?'

The Scientificky-sounding Long-range Weather Forecaster

John Fielding works for Weatheroid, a company specializing in providing long-range weather forecasts to the media, which they reproduce faithfully.

April and September are the busiest months. That's when I predict the WARMEST SUMMER EVER or 'We could be set for conditions as cold as Moscow this winter'.

You have to add a bit of science in, so for summer I say that it's El Niño or something around the Azores. And then for winter it's Eastern Siberia or the jet stream around Canada.

I put it up on Facebook and then the papers will get in touch and just do a copy-and-paste. Then they'll get some images of a cold winter from, like, ten years ago and put that in so people can really see what extreme weather looks like.

They'll probably get some proper weather forecaster to say it's a load of bull but that's usually at the end of the article and no one reads that far because they don't have the time.

I'm not the only one in this game. You'll have the old guy who watches nature, but he's just an amateur. He doesn't have it monetized like I do. He'll be watching to see whether the ferrets have umbrellas or if the swallows are trying to get their chicks privately educated or whatever culchie signs he sees. But mine has stats in it and sounds better.

And the best bit? It doesn't matter. The media never bother to check up on our predictions afterwards. I've done ten *Warmest Summer Evers* and twelve *Expect Record Snowfalls* in my career and I was only right once, but that's because I did the prediction at the same time as watching the actual weather forecast on the telly.

COMMERCIAL BREAK

The Boom is back but it needs a mascot!
We can't use a tiger because a tiger doesn't describe us when we get money.
For a start, a tiger has great timing.
You never see a tiger buying a ghost estate at the top of the market.
Vote for your Celtic Animal from the nominees below.

CELTIC BULLOCK

Lacks balls. Constantly
Searching for greener
pastures.

CELTIC SHEEP

Doesn't do much. Follows
other countries' lead, often
to the SLAUGHTER.

CELTIC CAT

Smaller version of the tiger.
Likely to end up at a neighbours'
looking to get fed.

CELTIC CYCLOPS

Visually impaired.
Brought down by the Greeks.

CELTIC TEABAG

Destined to end up
in hot water only
to be squeezed for
all it's worth.

Part Two

PUBLIC

6

A Game of
Two Clichés

ONCE THE PROVINCE of the one per cent (the one per cent who did Debating in school), public speaking has become far more democratic. We have lost our fear of the camera and the spectacle and, as a result, the private Irish are thrust into the spotlight to say a few words. Results vary from adorable to inspiring to bolloxological. One area has seen an explosion in oul talk: sport.

Since Cúchulainn struck the first penalty *down the throat* of a goal-keeping dog, sport in this country has not just been a matter of life and death; it has been far more clichéd than that.

The passion, the high stakes of that first recorded sporting event was evident in the heroic level of the verbal exchanges between those first protagonists.

Sport is a huge part of our national identity, whether it's our native sports or the ones we try to beat England at.

For years, across many sporting codes, doing things the right way and achieving success were scorned as getting above our station. We were synonymous with passion, heart and never giving up the fight. Or at least that's what the Englishmen would say, smirkingly, as they extinguished their cheroots with their pointy boots and then extinguished our dreams with one nod to their bowmen.

There was very little sport on the telly. Mysterious European soccer players would appear out of the haze on tiny black-and-white screens where it was impossible to distinguish between their shirt colours. We would find out about events that happened hours after the event itself. Live GAA coverage would start about thirteen seconds before the match began and the credits would roll just as supporters danced on to the pitch with their bad haircuts and ill-fitting clothes.

Rugby consisted of Ireland being brave for a while and then, at about the 60th minute, the natural order was restored and the players could be seen making the 'Pint?' gesture and lighting up a Silk Cut as the silky French cut loose all around.

Now, though, it's gone the other way. With the rise in professionalism and sponsorship, and an explosion in media coverage, sport is everywhere. Which means it's also the source of so much shite-talk, mangled language, hyperbole and hyperbole-oxology. And analysis – lots of analysis.

Our main sports are GAA, rugby and soccer. A few others pop up from time to time. Basketball was briefly a big deal but there's no tradition like there is in the playgrounds of America. The three outdoor basketball courts built here following a National Lottery grant in 1992 are used for teenagers to congregate and send nude Snapchats of themselves to the objects of their affection. Hockey sometimes turns up on the Olympics but no one can understand why they don't just straighten up and hit the fecking thing properly.

There is a great athletics tradition but a lot of people now prefer to run over obstacles and take the hardest, boggiest, rockiest route from A to B, doing endurance races with titles like HURT YOUR BODY FOR NO REASON and HERE'S A SLAP IN THE FACE and RUN THROUGH A BOG – WHY? JUST DO IT.

For all of these other sports, though, the amount of talk and hype is proportionate to the events that have taken place. In GAA, rugby and soccer there's just too much sportsing for the average 'consumer' to process.

Talksport – Then and Now

The language has changed over the years too:

Rugby – an oval lot of talk

Then	Now
'I remember a few of the guys on tour – Bender, Paddy Slatts, Simon Bants, Denis, Johnno Parkinson (he's in the Gulf now actually, does a lot of event stuff for some of the sheikhs) – tied Bill Scott to the bus and HAHAHAHA dragged him hahahaha and of course there was the time we had the whiskey in the water bottle for injuries. I remember the ref thought Gordo was concussed but he was absolutely trousered. Great days. Of course this was before the professional era. You wouldn't get away with that kind of thing now.'	'The goys are in the gym neow from the age of foor or foive, doing weights, eating special protein Liga-shakes. We need this if we're to compete with the loikes of the Ole Blacks. In fact I would say it has to stort in pregnancy. Too many babies are already being left behoind by the toime they're boorn. It's just a different spooort naow.'

GAA – all we hear is Radio GAA GAA

Then	Now
'We're taking this game very serious. A lot of the lads have been off the drink since Tuesday.'	'We've seen huge benefits since the compulsory mindfulness training three nights a week. But we need to work on our shot selection and our stats guys are looking at the power readings from the Fitbits to see where we can just gain those tiny percentages. At Junior B level, it's the fractions that make all the difference. And we would expect our players to delay having families, starting jobs or attending funerals as soon as the pre-season League friendlies start.'

Soccer – Word Cup qualifiers

Then	Now
'We were playing Poland so much we used to warm up at the same end.'	'Actually there's no guarantee any of this won't happen again.'
'The tickets appear to have ended up in the hands of a mysterious man known only as George the Greek.'	'Actually this could happen now too. And the sport mightn't just be soccer. It could be for the dressage as well. But thankfully we have the BEST FANS IN THE WORLD (see p. 114).'

How to Be a Soccer Pundit

The language of football punditry is a recognizable version of English but with many crucial differences. As well as all the clichés, there are some basic rules that prove useful when co-commentating.

Initial legal disclaimer

'For me' is to be added at the start or end of every sentence. It's a qualifier to let the audience know that this is only opinion and the pundit is therefore not legally responsible if the events or facts described turn out to be incorrect. For example:

> 'Well, for me, the lad has to do better there. He'll be kicking himself when he watches this back.'

> 'He's a top-top player*, for me.'

For more controversial situations, there is a further complication when the pundit will, while claiming responsibility for the comment he is about to make, also attempt to make it our responsibility (as well as assuring us of their trustworthiness (see Truth Be Told, page 269)).

> 'Well . . . You feel . . . For me, that's a red card. (If I'm honest.)'

---

*A top-top player is a player who can play a bit but, unlike a top player, has done it on the big occasions.

Plural proper nouns

Although thus far, to the best of our knowledge, each top-top player has only lived once and has not been reincarnated or cloned, it may sometimes be necessary to duplicate him when you are listing a number of top-top players and you can't think of enough names. Just name two and pluralize them. Also add 'your' to drag us into it again.

> 'Well, for me, the team is lacking a few top-top players – your Messis, your Iniestas.'

Suspicion of elaborate haircuts

It is a maxim of football that the trustworthiness of a footballer to deliver a big performance is inversely proportional to the complexity of his haircut. Unless the player has had the haircut for quite some time and is instantly recognizable with that big mop, chances are the time spent coiffing it was at the expense of time spent on the training pitch and quaffing power-smoothies. It is the duty of the pundit to indicate this suspicion gently as the game goes on.

> 'Well, the new haircut didn't do him much good there, did it, Dave?'

We're not gay

While the rest of the population has largely moved on, the footballing world remains terrified that any remark could leave them open to the implication they might be gay. This is because there are no gay people in the game whatsoever, apparently, so no one wants to be the first.

'He has it all, Simon. The balance, the speed . . . He's just a beautiful player.'

'Well, speak for yourself, Phil, haha. Wouldn't be my taste now, more of a ladies' man meself.'

[Everyone laughs a little too hard.]

Unusual tenses

Sport is one of the few forms of entertainment where replays are shown. Replays have an interesting effect on time. Even though the event has taken place in the past, because the replay is being shown now, the pundit should change the tenses to reflect this, often several times in the space of a sentence.

'For me, that should be 2–1. He has come in there at the back stick and I don't know what he thinks he's doing. Look at the gaffer. He will have been disappointed by what he's seen there because this will be something he will have had drilled into the team on the training pitch. If the winger has passed it there, then it's a present on a plate for the striker.'

Malapropping-up

On occasion, in the heat of the moment the pundit will coin a phrase that is sort of right but sort of wrong. A game may include a 'stone-wall penalty' that is not given. Although it's possible the pundit is comparing the injustice of the penalty-that-never-was to the Stonewall riots in 1960s New York, more than likely he meant a 'stone-cold penalty'. There have also been many 'one foul-swoops', which are worse than 'fell-swoops' as they have an odour about them. The crowd in the stadium, or players waiting to see the colour of the card, have been on 'tender hooks'. Bringing on a substitute should introduce a 'fresh set of impetus'. But maybe the sneering is misplaced here. Maybe the language is better for it. Phrases like these and others of their 'elk' add a richness that could never be achieved on purpose. Sometimes we can be too 'pacific'.

Reading is cheating

For the pundits back in studio, the key thing is to sound authoritative. This doesn't mean knowing what you are talking about. It means that what you know is all that is necessary to know at this stage. So, for example, a pundit will say something like 'Well, obviously we don't know a lot about this team', not because they haven't bothered their barney to look them up, but because it's not important right now. If the team has players that don't play in the English Premiership or in the Champions League, they are 'an unknown quantity'. In the absence of that, you just need a few good adjectives. Teams from small countries are generally 'plucky'. Unless it's Ireland in which case it's 'valiant'. Teams from the Big Countries will all be 'there or thereabouts'. And everyone else is a 'dark horse'. Some teams will be 'everyone's dark horse'. Which technically makes them 'favourites'.

Scrum Down

There's just as much bolloxology in rugby but a lot of it will go over your head. Literally, because the people involved are about six and a half feet tall.

They're good guys, though, and it's all good banter. It should be possible to bluff your way through the analysis if standing in a pub around Rugby Time. As no one fully understands all the rules of rugby it's OK not to know what's going on, but a few stock phrases will get you through most games: 'Ah, very flat'/'Referee! He's at it all day'/'Hands!'/'Roll away.'

Because fans are still primarily from the 'had-the-points-for-Medicine-but-did-Business-like-his-dad' end of the spectrum, you can also risk a bit of polysyllabism. So instead of 'Very slow, boys' you can get away with 'PEDESTRIAN' and you won't get funny looks.

You may find yourself socializing with the rugby fraternity and hopefully be in the presence of an endangered species known as an alickadoo. An alickadoo is the wartiest of stalwarts. He has been around the club for decades, has all the keys to the clubhouse, remembers the good old days of Jonno Kearney and Scadser Donnegan, two legendary centres and drinkers, hahaha. This was in the days before fitness and conditioning and smoking bans and there were no physical barriers to playing the game. All you needed was a Leaving Cert from a good school.

Unfortunately alickadoos are a dying breed as they are not making any more of them – a discontinued line, as it were. Even stalwarts now are eight feet tall and taking protein supplements to optimize their key-handling and drive their sponsorship-selling performance. But while they are still around, an alickadoo is a good man to talk to to get the low-down.

The thing to remember about rugby social gatherings is that, as a cohort, while they may not still run the country themselves, they know all the people who do. It's a good way of finding out all the open secrets that never make it into the media. Events are referred to obliquely with lots of euphemism.

'Well, he had a spot of bother a few years ago . . . Very messy business with a lassie. Luckily enough now, never went to the DPP. A bit of money changed hands, of course, but . . . you know . . . nearly ruined the poor bugger.

105

Good guy – doing very well for himself now, though.'

Or there will be stories of how two pillars of society are at each other's throats.

'Well, it's not the first person he's sued. Sued the father after, you know . . . a bit of a property deal went south.'

'Was that hard on your father?'

'No, not my father, *his* father.'

They are like taxi drivers without the car. At some point you will offer an opinion on a topic only to hear the juiciest of lead-lines: 'Of course, you know what happened *there*, don't you?'

GAAdvertising

The advertising industry and the GAA player have been uneasy bedfellows over the years. Most sports people are not sales people. They feel uneasy if some creative type tries to bring them out of their shell and express themselves for the camera.

And it's getting harder. GAA product endorsement long ago was quite simple. Hurlers were mainly used to sell farming products because it was the one bit of telly Big Pharma knew big farmers would watch.

Nowadays, the GAA player is supposed to be more cosmopolitan, so there is less evidence of them on the land. Instead, they are shown at the forefront of sports science, actively involved in product development and the testing of substances that will help them achieve their superhuman potential. They are often pictured in a grey-lit lab, fighting mental demons as they prepare to do battle against Fate and the tiny mathematical variations that can be the difference between glorious success and the type of failure that would give succour to the forces of evil.

Lads in a Lab   Meaningless Graphs   Hurler as expert consultant

GAAlic

Luckily, GAA players are immune to this sort of bolloxology. They can't be seen to be doing anything other than training, taking one game at a time and hopefully being there or thereabouts in the final shake-up. They have therefore developed a patois all of their own in order to talk to the media in a way that does not give *ANY indication that they are IN ANY WAY taking anything for granted.*

What they say	What they mean
'Lookit/I spose/janaw'	'Give me a second until I come up with a way of phrasing this in order to deflect the praise you've just given me.'
'They're a young team, they'll be back again next year.'	'A few of the older lads are currently in dispute with the manager, who won't be back again next year.'
'They pushed us all the way.'	'There was a bit of pushing at the throw-in.'
'We've a lot of respect for them . . .	'We've no respect for them . . .
'. . . and the way they play the game.'	'I've no knuckles left.'
'Yerra, I was lucky, I just found myself in a bit of space.'	'I intentionally created a good position for myself, using the skills I've spent my whole career developing.'
''Twas manly stuff.'	'Someone was waiting for me in the car park with a machete but there are no easy games at this level.'

You could make a *Mastermind* specialist topic of stock answers to speculative questions in GAA interviews.

Denis Doran, you're from Killeshandra and your specialist topic is All-Ireland victory speeches and post-match interviews, and your time starts . . . now.

What does this All-Ireland win make up for?
The long nights in January.

How many of ye were out there on the pitch?
There were 15 of us out there on the pitch.

That is incorrect. In fact there were 21 of you, not forgetting the lads who came on and did a job, also all those who have been on and off the panel since day one, pushing everyone to give 110 per cent.

What did they – meaning the 15 of ye out there on the pitch, the subs who came on and the lads who have been around the panel since day one, pushing everyone to give 110 per cent – do?

> *They stood up and were counted.*

At what point?

> *When it mattered.*

Who did you nearly forget?

> *Mrs Deegan and the ladies for all the chicken suppers after training.*

How many cheers?

> *Three.*

Where will you see us all?

> *Down below in Nan Dempsey's bar.*

How much craic will there be there?

> *Some.*

What did you not come here to do?

> *I did not come here to badmouth Mikey Cogan.*

Who else did you not come here to badmouth?

> *Anyone else on the County Board.*

What kind of stuff is in danger of being refereed out of the game?

> *Manly stuff.*

What did it come—

> *[BEEP]*

What did it come down to at the end of the day when all is said and done, once the ball was thrown in and tactics have gone out the window?

Whoever had the greater hunger.

C'mon Loo Class Gaels

You're nearly match-ready. There's only one lesson to learn. How to talk in a stadium toilet.

A. The man in shorts who realises how much has been splashing on his trousers all this time. **B.** The man who tries to hurry the others up. **C.** The man calling the ref some type of bollox. **D.** The man who remarks on the irony of queuing in a men's toilet – a situation more common in a women's toilet. **E.** The man who says this is where the big knobs hang out.

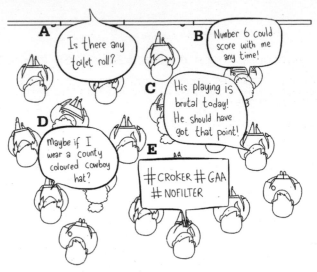

A. The woman who has realised there is no toilet paper after she's used the toilet. **B.** The woman rating the players on their attractiveness.
C. The woman berating the players on their performance.
D. The woman trying to get the GAA jersey and denim skirt combo to work
E. The woman taking a selfie because the lighting is really good so why wouldn't she take one?

Hyperball-e

The problem for sports media is that the actual playing time is much shorter than the time or space available. So a lot of sports media consists of reports on not a whole lot happening, and in-depth analysis on things that could be mentioned in passing, over a cup of tea and a biscuit.

> 'Joining us now for an hour to discuss the debacle in the Louth Under-14 league, where it appears that there is a discrepancy between the number of jerseys sent off to be washed and the number that came back, is Killbudigan's media relations manager, Johnny Myler.'

Sports hyperbole in the media is so ever-present that we probably have stopped noticing it. But let's try a little thought experiment*.

Take this normal situation:

Son: 'Mam, I cut my finger. Would you have a plaster?'

Mother: 'I do. Here you go.'

Son: 'Thanks, Mam. That feels better.'

Now pretend it's being reported by the sports press:

More Injury Misery For Wunderkind As Breadknife Hoodoo Strikes Again

IT LOOKS LIKE THE FAMILY breadknife has the Indian sign over O'Brien's star son Conor, as the 17-year-old starlet suffered a devastating setback once again while on the road to recovery from a previous bout of hang-nail. O'Brien's mother LAMBASTED the knife saying it was a divil and issued a call to other family members to exercise caution. 'This has been an accident waiting to happen and procedures have been lax at the organization for a while now.'

Holding back tears, Mrs O'Brien expressed the hope that no other family would go through the same heartbreak. She refused to be drawn on whether she would be instigating legal proceedings, asking instead for privacy at this difficult time, once the various social media outlets had been updated.

Conor was quick to pay tribute to medical staff, taking to Twitter to let friends know of his status and to reassure fans he was on the road to recovery.

---

*Bolloxologish for 'pretendy'.

113

The Irish Are The Best Fans In The World And If You Disagree We'd Fight You Only We'd Be Terrified Of Losing Our Title As The Best Fans In The World

BETHLEHEM 00

But we are, though. It's very hard to resist. You're on Facebook, minding your own and everyone else's business, and then you see it. A link that says: THIS VIDEO OF IRISH FANS HAVING THE CRAIC AND THE BANTER IS BREAKING THE INTERNET, FURTHER PROOF THAT IRISH FANS ARE THE

BEST IN THE WORLD AND WILL RESTORE YOUR FAITH IN HUMANITY. AND YOU WOULDN'T SEE THE ENGLISH LADS DOING THAT, OH NO.

Most of the videos are funny and heart-warming. It's that humour that's innate to the Irish fan. In Irish football, comedy is tragedy plus injury time. You are fully aware of the ever-present possibility of what George Hamilton would call *danger-here*.

It's hard to sneer at an impromptu performance of 'Rock The Boat' blocking a French street. Or the French builder with a combination of Gallic insouciance and cowboy attitude to health and safety, who carries about fifty fans in and on the roof of his pickup truck – as in 'Carlsberg don't do Cricklewood hiring fairs but if they did . . .' And try not to get teary watching the moment when Irish and Swedish fans applaud each other's team buses and then come together in the largest coalition of sweaty, euphoric, hugging, dancing men seen since the heyday of Studio 54. And Irish fans cleaning up after themselves in Bordeaux? Are you kidding?

It's turning into a bit of an arms race. What'll the fans do at the next championships in the spirit of banter? Deliver a baby? Or will their good-natured attempts at 'reaching out' be misinterpreted by Russian police, leading to a new Gulag full of Irish lads protesting that they were only having a laugh, like.

There's a bit of cranking from those who say that we try too hard to be liked in this country. What's wrong with being liked? We're a small country in an increasingly partisan world. Being liked might come in handy. We're defenceless. We're not Sparta. We sold our oil to yer man for some magic beans; our fish for a butter mountain. Paying 0.2 per cent corporation tax and likeability are key pillars of our Horizon 2030 plan for prosperity. These ambassadors in France may not have been handing out the Ferrero Rocher but they were spoiling us.

But, one word is a small cloud: viral. If a fan does something hilarious on tour and it doesn't go viral, did it really happen? Some videos are too self-aware (see page 262). Let's not make an industry out of Banter Ireland, Inc. Irish fans have been enjoying themselves for years but the total recorded footage from Euro '88 barely fills an episode of *Reeling in the Years* and four verses of a Christy Moore song. They were just in the moment. Locked, but in the moment nonetheless. That's the way it should be.

And that's the end of our comprehensive sports coverage. Oh wait – we nearly forgot the Olympics. That might need a separate book. And a team of lawyers (see Commercially sensitive, p. 275).

7

Hard to Swallow

THE FOOD COLONIZATION of Ireland has been similar to the waves of invaders we have endured over the centuries. The spud is our Tuatha Dé Danann. Although it's not native, it feels intrinsically Irish. It seems to match us. It's pinkish with blemishes, sunburns badly and is thin-skinned if you dig too closely around its roots. Prone to mushiness if left to wallow too long, it likes to go out, get absolutely mashed and lose its jacket. And, just like us, it looks like a potato.

But we have grudgingly allowed other foods to grace our land. Pasta is like the Normans. Treated with suspicion originally, it swiftly intermarried with the locals and blended in to the extent that it is often unrecognizable to its forbears who remained at home. Who can deny now that lasagne with chips is *more Irish than the Irish themselves*?

Every Irish town worth fighting over outside the pub has a Chinese restaurant. Chinese food too has adapted to fit us, with most dishes now being shovel-ready. And the discarded aluminium foil carton is as much a feature of Irish hedgerows as the dock leaf and the small pile of loose chippings left by the council after an early Friday-afternoon finish.

One by one, the non-sliced cheese, the Spanishy meat and the avocados have landed on our shores. Early on, they kept themselves to themselves, only peeping out tentatively in recipes in the weekend supplements. And then all at once they exploded, all over our faces. Pine nuts are now tossed into conversation like confetti. (In fact, for a healthy, safe alternative to throwing rice at a wedding, why not throw chia seeds? They're safer for the birds and will keep them going during a busy day of flying over and back for no reason.)

Given our drab past and lack of culinary tradition, when it comes to food we still have insecurities, which often leads us to overdo it. Effectively, there is a danger we have thrown the cabbage out with the cabbage water.

Eating Out of Hand

It's getting more and more difficult to find the sort of restaurant you'd bring your parents to. In the last decade there has been a tendency in culinary interior design to let you see the total inner-workings of the restaurant. Inspired by fly-on-the-wall documentaries, there is an expectation that the customer wants to see *everything*. You are shown the piping on the ceiling, while the lights hang down from metal cable ducts. The brickwork is exposed in the sideways-leaning room to show that the walls are real. Most new restaurants now resemble An Old Abandoned Warehouse At The Edge Of Town that could easily double as the setting for the climactic battle between Adam West's Batman and the villain. You can see right into the kitchen where the staff are hard at work. You can see tensions – aggression and romance – simmer between Emily, the feisty waitress, and Alvaro, the brooding sous-chef. Plus, there's usually a man welding together bits of an art installation in the corner.

But looking at all of this would exhaust you. Sometimes you need the right kind of notions – notions that are whispered and barely referred to. I have a dream. That one day a new restaurant will open that is *not* an 'eaterie'. That it will *not* replicate the feeling of eating in your own house while renovations are going on. I dream of a ceiling where ducts and untidy wires are safely tucked away behind the tiles. Instead of the waiter calling you 'man', they address you formally. I dream of a place where they take your coat. Where the menus are leather-bound, written in *Lucida Calligraphy* and not carved into old cereal boxes. A place that's not full of people telling each other that 'YOU SOOO HAVE TO WATCH IT? IT'S ON NETFLIX?' A place that's full of slightly tense conversations between rural parents and their adult children-with-notions – a father who looks like the father in the video for Cyndi Lauper's 'Girls Just Wanna Have Fun' and a bearded son who might have a long CV of 'dynamic roles' that didn't add up to a whole hill of black beans while his mammy just hopes he'll meet *someone*. And a conversation that goes something like this:

'Answer your father, Brian!'

'Dad, we've been through this. I'm not interested in taking over the business and I'm not Brian any more. I'm B7 — Design Disruption Guerrilla.'

'Well, B7, I don't care what kind of monkey you are, I need you on Monday morning at the warehouse to unload those pallets.'

'Dad, I've told you. I won't be there. I'll be in Berlin at the WHAT R OUI? conference.'

'That mash is lovely – so soft.'

'Don't mind the mash, Kay. So this clown doesn't want to go into the business. What have I spent the last twenty years building it up for if he wants to go off to his oul conferences?'

Mostly, I dream of a place with plates.

WHAT HAPPENED TO THE PLATES? They seemed to be perfectly serviceable vessels for food until someone felt the need to *disrupt* them. There's reason behind the saying, 'There's no need to reinvent the wheel.' The wheel is the product of millennia of honing. But it's still essentially round.

You know what else is round? A plate. Yet now, round

Ice cream servings in restaurants

1995

2005

2015

2025

2035

plates are an endangered species. It's not clear why. All manner of objects are now being used: everything from timber board to slate to shards of stained glass to buckets to dustpan sets. Is it all about aesthetics?

If a restaurant serves a burger on a piece of slate, are they telling you that you're not stuffing your face, you're part of a performance piece 'redefining our concept of burger'. Or are they emphasizing the 'artisanity'? When they serve chips in a little wire basket shaped like a lobster pot, perhaps they are saying, 'Look at our fresh wild chips, just caught this morning.' Mashed potato has been served in a little saucepan. It's only a matter of time before the bread arrives inside a small oven.

Design is all very well but there should be an opt-out clause. Here's a solution. You know the allergen list? Well, add a number to that: 16 – Bullshit food receptacles. Plates only please.

Cordon Blah

Food goes through phases of popularity. In another generation, the foods listed below will be endearingly rustic but at the moment some dishes are in danger of being over-plated. At the moment, they are enjoying a renaissance, or at least a naissance. But how did the actual Renaissance end? With the bloody chaos of the Thirty Years' War. All we're saying is: you can have too much of a good thing.

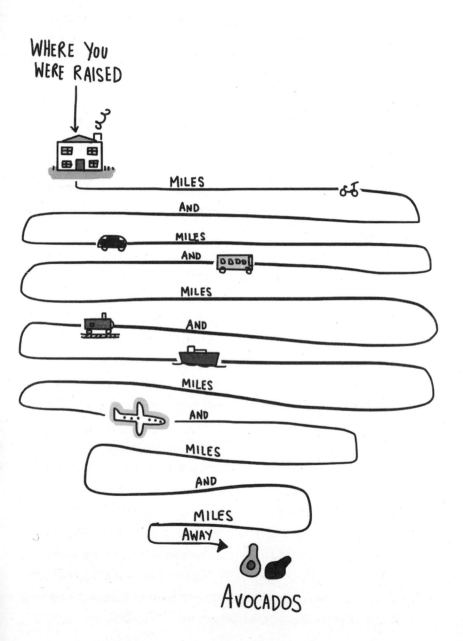

WHERE YOU WERE RAISED

MILES
AND
MILES
AND
MILES
AND
MILES
AND
MILES
AND
MILES
AND
MILES
AWAY

AVOCADOS

Black pudding

Speaking of blood, we reached peak black pudding in early 2016 when the World Health Organization proclaimed that black pudding is now not only *good* for you, but it is in fact a superfood. Its inexorable march continues and the sinister links between the black-pudding industry and the neo-conservatives are no doubt soon to be revealed.

Like a lot of elements of bolloxology, the black pudding, which is often qualified with the adjective 'humble', has its roots in a time when we didn't have a whole lot. The black pudding then on offer looked like a cross between a truncheon and a length of Wavin piping. When sliced and fried it could be used as pieces on a draughts board or as an ice-hockey puck. It was rarely seen outside a full Irish breakfast.

Thankfully, a number of enlightened companies decided that black pudding need not be awful. The first breakthrough came with the invention of the 'breakfast roll' by an engineering firm in Strokestown, Co. Roscommon. Black pudding was now in vogue.

These days, you can't move for it. It has displaced prawn cocktail and cream of vegetable soup as the Only Starter That's Any Way Nice on most restaurant menus but the quality has once again declined. Wagon wheels of the stuff now nestle on plates so covered in greenery they could form part of the Rural Environment Protection Scheme. And we lap it up because isn't it mad to get black pudding but not in a breakfast roll?

This is not a rant about black pudding as a food

or domestic consumption of black pudding. What consenting adults do in the comfort of their own homes is not a problem. Indeed, frying a black pudding so that it breaks down and then mixing it with beans – a meal known as 'filthy beans' – is perfectly acceptable.

But in starters in restaurants all across the bolloxological spectrum, black pudding needs a rest.

Butternut squash (and pumpkins)

We were always going to be suckers for it – it has 'butter' in its name. The Irish have just recently shaken off a dangerous flirtation with spreads to reclaim butter as a national emblem. And nuts: unless you've an allergy, who doesn't love nuts? There was a time when nuts were a perfectly acceptable Christmas present. Finally, the word 'squash' is just lovely. Remember running into the house at a quarter past two on a roasting summer's day, the smell of sunburnt skin in your nostrils, the match in the yard tied at 33-all? With any luck there was still a bit of squash left – MiWadi, yellow-pack, anything. Just dilute it with enough water to take the hydrocarbon taste off it and you were refuelled to go back outside until sunset, hunting rabbits or whatever it was we used to do.

So straight away the butternut squash was going to weasel its way into our affections. But the butternut squash has none of the elements its name evokes. It's bland; it doesn't taste like anything. It's orange, but not in a good way; more the colour that the walls in school were painted. You never see butternut squash standing solo on a menu. It always has to be part of something, like the most boring of your friends who insists on tagging along to every party. That's why you get Butternut Squash And A Load Of Other Stuff soups. You need to put in a lot of pepper.

Butternothing squash is joined by its fellow countryman the pumpkin, which came in as part of the bolloxification of Irish holidays such as Hallowe'en. Once we started hollowing out the thing, we started eating it as well. More orange soft mush. Just because the Native Americans ate it doesn't mean they liked it.

Potatoes at functions

Somewhere along the line we became embarrassed by the potato and so we made sure to try to disguise it as much as possible. That is why now, at the swankiest of dos, you can't just get a potato. It has to be gentrified into Potato à la Some Sort of French Royal Lineage.

The proud structure of the spud has been puréed into almost 80 per cent cream and a teaspoon of it has been dolloped next to the meat along with some vegetable trussed up in its own leaves.

Why not just give everyone a boiled spud in its jacket and a few for the table? The creamerati would probably protest, saying it would lead to disagreements at weddings and other functions; people would get different-sized spuds and there'd be tension over who would take the last spud out of the serving bowl.

Nonsense – it would help bring people closer together. Think of the last business lunch or dinner you attended. Did you struggle for conversation? Now imagine you are tussling over the last spud. You will never forget that connection: a business link made for life or a worthy rival.

Pulled anything

When future humans look back at the chronicles of the decline of civilization, they may trace one of the causes to a particular brand of fecklessness: our unwillingness to just chew the fecking meat like the animals we still are.

The pullvolution, which has seen the pre-chewing of innocent pigs, chickens and ducks, has taken away one of life's great pleasures – biting into a sandwich and removing most of the meat with your teeth while leaving the bread structure still in your hands. Now you are left scrabbling around on the floor for the meat scraps that get blown away by the slightest breeze.

Here's a recommendation for the future of meat: catch the animal, butcher it and then cut the meat into whatever size will fit on a round plate next to two boiled spuds. Let us do the pulling.

Any house burger

Maybe it's their propensity to provide a large window seat for witnessing various late-night fights, but there is a certain snobbery about chippers. They are at the vanguard of culinary culture. Or at least, at some point in the past they approached the vanguard of culinary culture, saw that it was a job well done and then left it well alone. However, one offering on the chipper menu has been neglected even by post-modern acolytes. The chipper burger.

Look, we know what we're eating when eating a burger. (Or at least we are clear about what we'd rather not know.) It's not foraged from a forest. It's not paleo. But a good chipper burger is all you need. The 'meat' is manageable. The bun is spongey and resilient with a texture not unlike carpet underlay but it *sticks together* and allows for lots of soakage.

However, the unending search for growth has seen the height of burgers elsewhere increase. Some expansion was welcome but there is a law of diminishing returns when you measure the size of the burger against the degree of enjoyment experienced.

Some burgers look like they could be used as a *Man v. Food* challenge in a midwest American town that has lost most of its heavy industry to lower-wage economies. While eating them, one flirts with lockjaw.

Conversely, there has been *no* advance in bun technology in recent years – the bun will inevitably collapse mid-burger, leaving you with a fingertip-sized piece of bread on either side of a mound of meat. You end up finishing the burger much as though you'd salvaged it from the food bin. Or worse – you have to eat it with a knife and fork. If you wanted to eat macerated meat with a knife and fork you would have ordered the pulled pork. It's a thoroughly joyless experience.

The same goes for hand-cut chips. One hopes they're hand-cut if they're charging five euro for them, but could they do a bit more cutting? Hand-cut chips or home fries have grown to the size of half potatoes. Unlike pulled pork, we like our chips pre-chipped. That seems intrinsic to the name. Again, restaurants need to ape the local chipper. In fact, they should just run out the door and buy the chips from the nearby chipper and bring them in to us. They can even wrap them in their stupid, pretend newspaper if they want and serve them on a dustpan or in the bucket of a Tonka Mighty. Just bring chipper chips.

Loos Talk

Restaurants and pubs establish their visual identity in many ways but one thing they should leave alone is the toilet door. When you are running to it in an emergency, you need to know very quickly which gender it is.

What you don't need is to waste valuable seconds trying to decipher what the hell the designer or the 'quirky' owner had in mind when they put their cryptic symbols on the doors. What's so wrong with the bog-standard male or female silhouettes?

In Ireland, 'fir' and 'mná' are acceptable, unless

HANDCUT SANDWICHES

HANDCUT CHIPS

HANDCOOKED CRISPS

Yanks are going to think we spelled 'man' wrong. Or unless just 'M' and 'F' are used, which gets really confusing. What are *not* acceptable are convoluted signs representing male and female – in one example a rooster and a cat. One punter was reported to have nearly had an accident while trying to work out the joke. (Cocks and pussies, since you asked. You're sorry you did.)

What about those for whom English is a second language? How are they supposed to know, when confronted with the toilet doors in a giant barn of a Monaghan pub-disco, what a colt and a filly are?

Where is this going? Will we see adjacent toilet doors with two blackbirds on it and you're supposed to know that the female is the duller brown colour while the male has a yellow beak? Or two walruses and you have to measure their size to know which is which?

There is a saviour from an unlikely source. The growth in awareness of those for whom gender is not binary means there will be more gender-neutral toilets. Also, there probably won't be enough imagination to come up with inoffensive puns for these toilets, so we may gradually see sanity restored to the toilet-door world. So, if you're someone who likes taking a pop at those for whom gender is not straightforward, remember to thank them in future when you dash to the facilities in Club Destiny, the Town's main nightclub, and don't have to decipher 'hombres' and 'mujeres'.

Beyond the Paleo

Paleo diets and primal living are the latest lifestyle fads. There is a tendency to romanticize our ancient forefathers, to fetishize the simplicity and nobility of their lives.

We imagine a wise, bearded man, leaning on a staff and gazing over a valley, a braided-haired woman at his side with a couple of Kinder-Bueno children scuttling around the savannah. The message is that the Ancients were better than us and have so much to teach us for the following reasons:

- **They didn't work in offices.** The world was their office. They had their status meetings in the forests with one item on the agenda: What are we hunting to ensure our survival today? There were no blame-storms or lessons learned. If the buffalo hoof-print on your temple didn't teach you, nothing would.

- **They didn't eat processed foods.** Nestling in their bellies were grains, berries and some scavenged meat from the decomposing corpse of an animal that also ate grains and berries and foraged in the undergrowth, an animal that also led a noble existence. If it was hunted by the Ancients, it looked them in the eye, saluted with a paw and said, 'It's a fair cop, guv.'

- **They stare out at us from that article on the internet about How We Have Lost Touch With Our Past Selves**, hunched over our computer screens, a breakfast roll in our hands, ketchup dripping on the keyboard. We are guilty. Guilty of being slaves to the military-industrial complex and the relentless Big Breakfast Roll lobby.

- **Their tousled-hair children ran free and explored nature**. They made friends with a stoat back when all the animals were friends. They poked at something with a stick. Look at your whiny spawn with their expectations and entitlements, their soft feet and their vaccinations and their matching outfits. And that's just the university students going on gap years.

- **They could do stuff.** They could whittle and make a shelter out of dock leaves and catch a sparrow with a trap fashioned out of back hair. And what's your skill? You know how to watch *Game of Thrones* for free on the website that keeps changing its domain name to stay ahead of the FBI, and how to avoid clicking on links that cause viruses.

They're looking back at you, these paleos, these primal humans, these Ancients. And do you know what they're thinking? They're thinking, 'That breakfast roll looks very nice. Why am I wasting my time foraging for wild grains, competing with warthogs and telling the children to look out for giant sloths?'

The paleos ate what they did because they didn't have a choice. It wasn't the paleo diet to them. It was just food. We know what they ate because we've found some of their bodies and analysed the contents of their stomachs. Those bodies were in a bog where no doubt they were dumped after being sacrificed when a hunt failed. And their children were then probably sold to Niall of the Nine Hostages. Think about that.

Eat your breakfast roll with pride. It's progress. Ring a Man when something breaks. Pick your child up when they cry and spoil them and spend four years getting them to sleep in their own bed.

Yes, you're soft as f*ck and you'll probably be the first to die when the apocalypse comes; but really, do you want to survive the apocalypse and have a load of Bear Gryllses for company, giving out to you for not eating your grubs? Consider the surviving characters of *The Walking Dead*. How many of them would you actually like to spend the End of Days with?

And while you're at it, ignore any oul medical stuff whose only selling point is that that's what the Ancient Chinese did. Chinese medicine also suggests you should treat impotence with ground-up tiger 'parts'. Lookit, go down to the chemist and they'll give you something. Take two aspirin with your fructose-saturated bun. You'll be grand.

Coffeelloxology

We get it. You love your coffee. You can't start the day without it. You've said it repeatedly: *I just can't function without my coffee.* Good luck to you.

Caffeine has many proven benefits. It has been a staple of many societies for a thousand years, ever since an Ethiopian goat-herder noticed that his flock seemed to *lose all critical faculties* and were quite happy to queue for ages to nibble the berries of the shrub Coffea arabica. Your rights to coffee do not necessarily infringe on others'. If you want to spend a few grand a year on mocha-choca-semi-skimmed-skinny-full-fat drinks made with beans pre-digested by Vietnamese polecats, you have every right.

Except where those rights *do* infringe on the rights of others. Your insistence on swanky coffee means it takes too long to make it in the café. There are other people in the queue with simpler tastes who need to get to work in order to make up for the productivity you're losing with your complicated beverage.

Below is a solution that should satisfy everyone. You can go and queue with your aficionados. The rest of us who have somewhere else to be can get our fix in a fraction of the time. It's a café with two very distinct zones. One for Tea-Tea and one for all the other shite.

8

The Dhrink

WHEN IT COMES TO BOLLOXOLOGY, drink is a double-edged sword. In some cases it has even led to incidents with double-edged swords. Drink loosens the tongue and pretensions can be exposed:

'Where we ye before this?'
'Like, Witch Hazel and Corncrake?'
'Where?! G'way outta that, ya langer. What did you have? The patronized kumquat? Haha.'

Although when there's more drink taken, fairly ordinary things can be unfairly, almost absurdly criticized.

'Where did you get the jumper?'
'Dunnes.'
'DUNNES! Oh lah-di-dah.'

We are obviously in denial about our alcoholism but when it comes to drinking, maybe some perceptions of the Irish can be a little unfair. Amidst all the excuses that there is something in our psyche that tends to melancholy (or the weather or oppression or the Church), when we rationalize our drinking, we ignore one fact. Sometimes we drink just so we can give full vent to one of our 450 words to describe being drunk. Listen to any Irish person report what kind of a state poor Johnny or poor Tracey – and she can't handle it *at all* – got into the night before and you will hear an effusiveness that is absent from the rest of the conversation.

> 'Oh, lads*, I was feckin' LOCKED OUT OF MY BISCUIT/hammered/trousered/scuttered/in tatters/in flitters/stocious. It was carnage. Out of my MIND with drink.'

You could make up your own word by simply taking any noun and adding '-ed' after it. Look around you. What do you see? Now put it into a sentence:

> 'I was floored, ceilinged. I was PARTITIONED last night. Inkjetted. Absolutely desk-topped. Timmy was worse – he was completely cubicled.'

You get the picture.

Every syllable must be enunciated. Such enthusiasm for vocalizing what was probably a fairly average night can lead to choosing words for being drunk that might not have great connotations.

We're always using geopolitical situations to describe our drunkenness: 'OMG – I was blitzed last night.' In

*When drink is involved, both genders can be addressed as male.

other words, I was so drunk at Donal's leaving drinks, it was the equivalent of being bombed by the Luftwaffe. 'Tuesday night was feckin' Fallujah, lads.'

So Real

The word 'authentic' is laden with Bx. It places huge pressure on you when you go on holiday. It's imperative to have the authentic local experience or the whole holiday is completely worthless. Don't go to Starbucks. Find the tavern that only seats four people, one of whom is an old woman still cleaning the rifle with which she once shot four Nazis who were menacing her goats. Drink the liquid made from fermented mule's milk. Watch uneasily as your twelve-year-old is guided into another room and subjected to a vaguely dangerous initiation ritual involving knives. Job done: now you can relax. You can go to McDonald's for the rest of the trip safe in the knowledge that you've got the authentic monkey off your back.

Thankfully, in Ireland you're spared the need to eat in an authentic Irish restaurant, so the search for authenticity only extends as far as the Irish pub. What Irish pubs actually bring to the table is lighting and seating. Irish pubs are dark, allowing the kind of anonymity you need for the shared experience. You see pubs and cafés in places like Spain that are so bright that drinking in them feels like sneaking a few sups out of a bottle of Harp in a grand-aunt's kitchen, after a removal on a summer's night in 1988. And Irish pubs have comfortable chairs. Once you have that, that's all you need. But if you must be 'authentic', proceed with caution.

The words 'authentic' and 'Irish pub' have been abused in the past. In fact, they shouldn't be used in the same sentence. Authenticity is extremely rare and when you go looking for it, past experience tells it to retreat in fear, like a corncrake. Indeed, the Quantum Law of Authenticity states that authenticity can only exist when it's not observed.

The Irish pub has been through a few waves of bolloxology and, as each one has retreated, it has left its mark. Complaining about the lack of authenticity in Irish pubs abroad is like complaining that the *Murder She Wrote* episode set in Ireland did not offer a nuanced portrayal of a country at a crossroads between European modernity and post-colonial identity rebuilding. They are only 'authentic' in the way that Tom Cruise's *Far and Away* accent was 'authentic'.

A lot of lyrical waxing has been done about the intangible qualities that make the Irish pub a superior night-time venue. Some have spoken about the 'craic'. (See The Craic, page 272, for more on this.) The craic, like authenticity, has to be approached carefully. You have to find it without appearing to look for it. Irish pubs employ a number of strategies to create the ideal conditions for the craic.

The right music

Music is one of the greatest sources of bolloxology in an Irish pub, so a tricky path has to be navigated through it.

Most common is the trad session, which typically involves a man in the corner, hunched over a squeeze-box, with a pint on the table and another stored somewhere in his beard, playing Planxty's 'Modem' and the 'Ghost Estates of Tullamore'. This has its place, but there should be decorum. You shouldn't have to whisht everyone else in the pub just to hear yet another ballad about a man who was cruelly betrayed to the English by a red-haired woman.

But you can't just magic up a trad session. Some places don't even have enough musicians around. Pubs are under pressure these days from all sides. The smoking ban has driven some ould lads away, the last of the professional smokers who wouldn't be caught dead vaping. For the price of a pint you can get a tanker full of Devil's Pelvic Girdle Cider in the off-licence.

So publicans have to do something to get a bit of atmosphere going. Many have diversified into food and craft beer (see page 144). Food can only last so far into the night, though, and craft beer is itself leading to a decline in the amount drunk, as you spend a good bit of time trying to figure out which local beer to try: Bottle Blonde Ale or 1921 Reprisal Shooting Pilsner?

Atmosphere, like craic and authenticity, is difficult to manufacture. For a planet to be habitable, you need photosynthesis, volcanic eruptions spewing out vapours and an ionized magnetic field. Creating atmosphere in a pub is just as hard. You can't just conjure up a Bulmer's 'Nothing Added but Time' advertisement out of nothing. They don't grow on trees, those thirtysomething men with ironic plaid caps and woolly waistcoats, who look like Michael Fassbender (but not the way he looked in the 'dirty film'), flirting with women from a Vintage Baking Blog. You know the sort – the kind of people who lived in Budapest for a while but are home now.

While waiting for these types to arrive, the publican may try to get the place livened up by hiring The Man With The Keyboard. Spare a thought for him, in the corner of the pub, plugging in leads and setting up stands, a forced smile on his face: he is one of the true heroes of bolloxology. You rolled your eyes as he began to assemble his gear. You cursed him. You may even have left the pub altogether. But The Man With The Keyboard soldiers on in the face of such adversity. See him now, dressed in black trousers and a short-sleeved pink shirt, crooning 'Ring of Fire', 'Folsom Prison Blues' and some rather downbeat versions of Joe Dolan songs.

But next time he starts up 'Do You Want Your Old Lobby Washed Down?' and you have to shout to make yourself heard, don't grimace in his direction. You don't know who he is. He may not always have been The Man With The Keyboard. He could once have been in a wedding band that was all the rage years ago. But as time went on, the band broke up when demand for waltzes was replaced by demand for songs about the kind of state Rihanna or Azealia Banks would leave you in if you didn't measure up.

Anyway, some people like The Man With The Keyboard. They weren't planning on talking anyway. They don't need to have a discussion about what season two of *True Detective* was like. They want to sip a pint – Herself'll have a Cidona – and hear just why Muirsheen Durkin's friend seems to be so sick and tired of workin'.

And The Man With The Keyboard knows that, a few pints later, you'll be sidling up, asking for 'Galway Girl' and dancing around like an eejit. The Man With The Keyboard knows. Atmosphere is here at last.

Pints of viewing

People underestimate the importance of having a telly in an Irish pub. Not too many, mind. American bars have so many it's like drinking in Power City. Too much choice will make you unhappy.

The optimum number of televisions is two or three and, ideally, at least one of them should be one of those old 1980s wooden boxy ones, sitting precariously on a shelf that's so high you'd get a crick in your neck looking at it. If there are no televisions, then the place will be invaded by millennial types seeking 'authenticity'.

I Don't Know Much About Artisan But I Know What I Like

We've all been there. The bleary eyes. The previous night could be described 'a heavy one'. Some drinking took place but not a ruinous amount. It was just a night of good company and talk. Although, according to World Health Organization standards, it was technically an episode of binge drinking. Sure, what would they know? How could you go on a session with one of them lads? Sitting there in their white coats, looking at you judgementally with their binge-o-meter. How do they expect Irish males to progress a conversation past 'Did you see the match last night?' if we're afraid of tipping into binge territory as soon as we get warmed up?

But then you remember something that immediately makes you feel better. *I was drinking craft beer.* This put a whole new complexion on things. A hangover after a night on one of the multinational brands makes you feel dirty. You've once again been manipulated by their insidious advertising campaign involving a man-child doing a silly dance or running down a snowy mountain. But drinking *craft* beer? That's practically an act of patriotism. Since each pint takes one person a year to hand-carve, every one you drink creates a whole job. Contrast that with the non-craft variety where a tree is cut down just for the sheer badness of it.

Craft beers do give you a hangover but because they're so artisan, the pain is more rustic, like the backache you'd get from hours spent digging for truffles on a hillside in the Auvergne.

Once the province of bearded pubs, craft beers are slowly colonizing the traditional locals. Somewhere, a publican – the kind who would wipe the knife used to butter the white sliced pan (and level the top of a pint) off the back of his trousers – is looking suspiciously at a bottle of Devil's Collarbone ale. 'We're just after getting this stuff in,' he tells you. (They bought six bottles.)

'Would you try it? It's supposed to be all the go above in Dublin.'

But the craft-beer industry has one problem that is a mark of its success: there's too much choice. It used to be possible to go into an off-licence and on the wall of cans were the ones you saw on the telly and the ones you saw dumped next to the canal. You had a very simple value judgement to make. Did you want the can that says 'Hey, dude, wanna drink some dude-beers?' or 'HEY, YOU, SCUTMONKEY, DRINK ME BECAUSE I'M ALL YOU HAVE'.

Now, though, we are presented with so much choice we are paralysed. There'll be just five bottles of each beer as the off-licence experiments. Some choices are easy. Do I want to spend €4.90 on a thimbleful of Ploughman's Nectar – thrice-brewed, drained through a ferret's gizzard, infused with kale? Probably not.

But elsewhere there is a visual cacophony of folksy or Victoriana labels promising outlandish concepts in beer like 'body' and 'taste'. Your throat goes dry (or drier). The beer you had last week is gone. You were just getting attached to it but obviously you were the only one and it didn't sell so now it has been replaced with some other concoction named after a megalithic dolmen.

Hurry up! It's 9.55pm and the staff are poised, ready to close the off-licence area. There is major panic. You grab something named after one of the lesser-known Fianna heroes and run out. You know you'll hate it. It will taste of *too much*. You're drinking to forget, not drinking to wonder what 'aroma' is going to explode at the back of your palate or how well it will go with duck.

The middle classes of beer have been hollowed out. It's either two-litre plastic bottles of AH F*CK OFF cider at one end or The Furze of the Weasel at the other.

The craft-brewing industry is still developing. Artisan beer-makers will know that they have truly arrived when their bottles are found dumped in bags at scenic locations. In order to make serious money, your product has to be bought by arseholes as well.

If you look here, you can see our brewery run by Artisants!

Authentic Microbrewing

9

That Shower, the Other Shower, Scattered Showers

THERE IS BOLLOXOLOGY ON BOTH SIDES when it comes to politics. As the electorate, we want our politicians to be the kind of people who can make speeches like they do in the films that end with 'Today is the dawn of a new republic, one where we are all equal under the law!' and also get a medical card for Nan because although she's technically over the income limit . . . still though, ah do.

The problem for politicians is that a lot of the time, they can't say what's really on their mind because either:

A. They were told: whatever you do, say nothing.

B. There is nothing to say.

C. It's their fault and they can't admit it because there's someone else looking for their job.

D. It's actually not that big a deal but it would take too long to explain and by the time they did, the public would be distracted, off checking their phones.

E. They *are* part of the Bilderberg Group, the Illuminati and the New World Order and this *is* a big conspiracy to strip the plebs of the last vestiges of control they had over their own lives so that the world can revert back to feudal times and ready itself for the Final Lizard Takeover.

F. They don't know the answer and they don't want to look stupid.

But, having said that, some politicians enjoy talking Bx a little *too* much.

How Most Interviews Go

Before the interview

INTERVIEWER:
And how are ye getting on with Public Sector reform?

MINISTER:
Ah! Don't talk to me about that. I'd love to burn the whole thing down. But that would be a bit of an Industrial Relations issue. Haha.

INTERVIEWER:

We're going to be asking you obviously about the political appointments scandal and the broadband scandal.

MINISTER:

Grand so – you know the craic. Do your worst, haha.

During the interview

INTERVIEWER:

Minister, there is a lot of concern about the political appointment scandal.

MINISTER:

Thank you first of all for the opportunity to speak to the Irish people on such an important topic. It is of paramount importance that there is utmost clarity with respect to the matter at hand and furthermore, I want to reaffirm my government's commitment under the auspices of the programme for government to be able to communicate in a way that is clear and concise and addresses the matter at hand, but also the issues which we are encountering time and time again as we go around the constituencies and hear from the grass roots – the man on the street, the mother who has watched her son emigrate, the GAA team that cannot play in a county-league game due to lack of numbers – these are the people that I am here to represent, who

151

don't have a voice at the top table. And that is my commitment to this situation at hand, at this point in time, in the fullness of time. Going forward.

INTERVIEWER:

So ... what about the political appointments scandal whereby the Junior Minister's son was made a special advisor even though he's only eight?

MINISTER:

Well, before I answer that, what I would say is that, if you'll let me finish. We have been given a mandate to do a job of work and that job of work for which we have been given the mandate is not completed yet. A job of work is far more complicated than normal work because effectively you have to do two things. The job and the work.

INTERVIEWER:

OK, Minister, but if I could ask you about the recent scandal involving political appointments—

MINISTER:

Well, obviously I can't comment on individual cases but we are in the business of making decisions and these decisions have to be made in the national interest.

INTERVIEWER:

You haven't answered the question—

MINISTER:

I will answer the question if you give me a chance to answer the question. Now you asked me about a scandal involving political appointments but in fact, we are committed to ensuring the best outcomes for the public, using best-of-breed methodology and in line with OECD norms and you'll see that this government has a proud record in that regard and a far better record of openness and clarity and procedures than the last government, which might I remind you made us the basket case of Europe.

INTERVIEWER:

But about this particular scandal? You are still not—

MINISTER:

Look, you can play word games all you want and actually this speaks to another point I'd like to make. The people and – let me tell you this, because I think it's important to make this point at this juncture – there is a disconnect between the concerns of the Dublin media and the ordinary people of Ireland. What the man and woman on the street are concerned about are their own jobs.

INTERVIEWER:

But is it not possible for them to be concerned about their own jobs *and* also annoyed about cronyism within the government?

MINISTER:

We are very serious about clamping down on cronyism. It was part of the mandate we were given and of course I understand their concern and let me tell you in the heel of the hunt, that is what I am concerned about and the people have elected me to do that.

INTERVIEWER:

But you haven't done anything about the cronyism – it's still going on!

MINISTER:

As I have said already we have a job of work to do and when this government came to power, unemployment was 15 per cent, we had three months' money left to pay the teachers and since this time we have . . .

INTERVIEWER:

But, Minister—

MINISTER:

And can I also say, and what I would say . . . that Foreign Direct Investment—

INTERVIEWER:

OK, Minister, we'll move on to the scandal of four hundred million that was spent on a broadband feasibility study and all that was produced was a one-page document on which was written 'Shur, chance it, but the reception is cat malogen*'. Will you now admit that the government needs to apologize and take responsibility?

MINISTER:

I am happy to take responsibility if it is deemed necessary.

INTERVIEWER:

So are you going to?

MINISTER:

But I have just said that I am happy to take responsibility.

INTERVIEWER:

If who deems it necessary?

MINISTER:

Well, that's not for me to say. I can't pre-empt any other discussions that are ongoing – as you well know . . .

INTERVIEWER:

Minister, I'm afraid we're out of time, thank you.

*Alternative spellings include 'cat melojen', 'cat melodeon' and 'cat malodgeon' but whichever way you spell it, it's pure cat altogether.

After the interview

MINISTER:

Well, lads, I thought that went well. I thought we only had three minutes. Ye nearly caught me, haha.

INTERVIEWER:

Yes, Minister.

Game of Drone

It's time to face facts. Most interviews with government politicians on news programmes are pointless. They're just a two-part play.

The politician has nothing to say until they figure out how to fix This Thing That Went Wrong. Or cover it up enough to tide them over until the next problem comes along. But they still have to do the interview because the media demands it and we the people have to sit through the Bx when we might as well be watching *The Chase* on ITV7 (or whatever number they're up to now). After a while they just sound like this:

INTERVIEWER:

BARK BARK BARK THE THING BARK BARK

POLITICIAN:

SOOTHE SOOTHE Let's be clear, stats that are not relevant, two billion SOOTHE SOOTHE

INTERVIEWER:
BARK BARK YOUR COLLEAGUE SAID SOMETHING
ELSE BARK BARK

POLITICIAN:
SOOTHE SOOTHE Well, obviously, that's a matter
for . . . SOOTHE SOOTHE

INTERVIEWER:
BARK BARK BARK THAT OTHER THING BARK
BARK

POLITICIAN:
SOOTHE SOOTHE . . . prejudice the outcome of the
inquiry SOOTHE SOOTHE

In an ideal world it should be possible to pre-interview
every politician over the phone just to see whether
there's any point in conducting the interview:

INTERVIEWER:
Well?

POLITICIAN:
Ah, it's a mess. I made a bollix of it because I'm not really
qualified for it and the civil servant who was supposed
to advise me is hanging me out to dry on this one because
I tried to clip his wings last year on another matter, so
I'm out of my depth, really. I'll need another couple of

days to figure out even what the problem is but I'd say I'll have to break my election promise for a start. It was stupid to make that promise because no one believed me anyway and I made it without knowing any of the facts.

INTERVIEWER:
What'll I tell the people?

POLITICIAN:
Tell them I'm sorry. I'm working on it. I'm an auctioneer. I don't know anything about Credit Default Swaps and promissory notes and hospital waiting lists but when yer man forgives me, I'll have a better idea. Tell them hang on a while and play music or go for a walk or something.

INTERVIEWER:
Grand so – any good news? What about those jobs? Do you want to claim credit for them?

POLITICIAN:
Well, there's a jobs announcement but they were already announced before the election so it'd be a waste of time. Honestly now, just cut the programme in half and show one of David Attenborough's programmes, maybe the one about the Arctic.

This will never happen, but one of the bolloxologies we are most prone to is trying to identify what exactly we want from our senior politicians. Obviously, not trousering friends' money in exchange for planning changes would be a good thing but no one ever gives them a job description.

How many mistakes should they be allowed to make? Should it be OK for them to change their minds? Is it time for the first act of a new minister to include a ceremonial burning of promises and then a statement about what is actually possible?

The Dáily Grind

Then again, our expectations are lowered by what happens when there are no interviewers around – when they're in the Dáil . . .

OPPOSITION TD:

A Cheann Comhairle, I'd like to ask the Minister in the light of . . . *[fifteen-minute preamble to ask the question which highlights the previous record of this and successive governments, followed by a question which could have been asked fifteen minutes ago]*

MINISTER:

A Cheann Comhairle, before I respond . . . *[fifteen-minute preamble highlighting how the questioner has had a different position on this in the past, alluding to recent strife within the party, throwing in a crap joke]* . . . but I take the deputy's point and can I just say that . . . *[mention work done in a different area, use some facts and figures, perhaps add up the total money spent on something over a long enough period of time so that the word 'billion' can be used]*

ANOTHER OPPOSITION TD:
[Playground-level heckle like 'You'd know all about that']

GOVERNMENT TD:
[Playground-level heckle like 'Your mother']

CEANN COMHAIRLE:
[Bell, exasperation, some obscure rule]

Seanacism

The Seanad is Ireland's upper house. It's in a smaller room than the Dáil and the atmosphere is a little calmer because if you're shouting abuse, you're much nearer the person you're abusing. The lighting is brighter, giving the impression that this is a calm, measured, high-brow area where people debate as if they were A Council Of The Elders Of Hibernia in a futuristic Ireland.

Only a few people get to vote in Seanad elections. While most of the world is familiar with the notion of a secret ballot, the Seanad might as well have a secret *election* because no one knows it's going on.

The Seanad electorate are as follows:

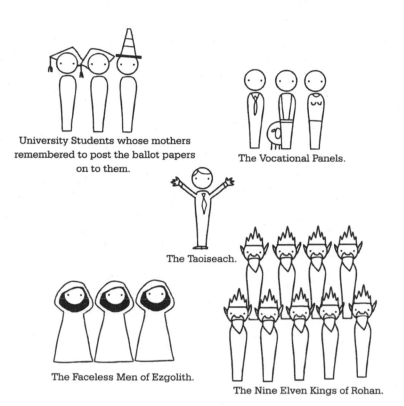

University Students whose mothers remembered to post the ballot papers on to them.

The Vocational Panels.

The Taoiseach.

The Faceless Men of Ezgolith.

The Nine Elven Kings of Rohan.

This means you can get a few wildcards in there. Former TDs or people who could never get elected in the 'real world' find a warm, welcoming bosom in the Seanad. And while the world worries about apocalyptic terrorists, you can always rely on a rogue senator to call for a ban on Pokémon Go or seagulls or weak tea. There was a referendum to abolish the Seanad recently but people rejected the proposal on the basis that although they weren't quite sure what it did, it might come in handy for something. In much the same way as you would hold on to a bit of string.

Sorrynotsorry: How to Apologize in Politics

A politician's apology is like a crème brûlée. You think you'd like one but once you get it you wonder why you bothered asking for it. The country waited years for an apology for the last economic debacle and when it was received it was a massive disappointment.

In normal English an apology should go something like this:

> 'Here's the thing I did. I am sorry I did it. I did it because of some failing in my character. It won't happen again. Here's some reparation to make up for it.'

However, no political spin doctor worth their salt would ever let their client say something as naive as this. Much better that they take a bolloxological approach, such as:

- **'I take responsibility.'** This is a great one to use in Ireland because no one actually has ever said what 'taking responsibility' means. The last people to do it regularly were the IRA, who used to claim responsibility, and they were all released under the Good Friday Agreement. So it's easy to see why you wouldn't take taking responsibility seriously.

- **'We found ourselves in government.'** Politicians will campaign strenuously for your vote, negotiate long into the night on a programme for government acceptable to all coalition partners and then express surprise that they happen to find themselves in government. As if it were an accident of Fate, that the universe conspired to force them into that situation, like an innocent mouse wandering into an alleyway filled with feral cats.

- **'For any pain that may have been caused.'** With this, you're already casting doubt on whether there was pain. Also, using the passive voice implies that it was caused not by the politician, but by the universe.

- **'I apologize if people took offence.'** This is a variation on the previous one. In other words, if someone was misguided enough to be offended at what was said, then, theoretically, an apology is available for them to claim. Provided of course they have filled out the correct paperwork. And that's now covered by a different department and they *[looks at clock]* are probably closed for lunch now.

- **'We took some hard decisions.'** As long as guaranteed pensions for ministers exist they will never have to take any truly hard decisions.

- **'It's important to move on now and learn from the mistakes of the past.'** Get over it, will you? And don't do it again.

If

If anyone was offended by what you said
Then in the course of time you will
Of course offer an apology
If one is necessary
If it is proven that you have done something wrong
That you knew was wrong anyway
And if you are caught
If the economic conditions are favourable and
If a newspaper draws attention to this election promise
That you made
If it's not for you to say
If it's not about you but about the people of this country
If Ireland is to sit at the top table of
Foreign Direct Investment
Then, my son, you are a man
We can go into coalition with.

(*With apologies to Rudyard Kipling, should he need any.*)

Electionese

A general election is the World Cup for politicians. There's a huge amount of airtime, some people who aren't normally on the telly get on and there's always a possibility of own goals.

Doorstep aside

'What we are hearing on the doorsteps' is a great get-out for the average politician. No matter what question is put to them, they can claim that that is not what they are hearing on the doorsteps. There could be poisonous gas in the atmosphere, zombies roaming the streets – and that's just the canvassers – but when it is put to the politician they can say, 'That is not what we are hearing on the doorsteps.' This is because no one has bothered to note which doorstep said what and therefore, there is no way of proving them wrong.

The main thing that is being heard on the doorsteps is:

> 'Oh, right . . . The election, is it . . . Well, I'll take a leaflet anyway . . . Sorry, I've a small baby to put to bed . . . OKbyenow, bye.'

We may swear we are going to give the politicians a piece of our mind but when faced with an actual human being on the doorstep, most of us freeze up and act all polite.

'Doorstep' also leaves out all apartment dwellers. There are, as yet, no documented instances of politicians saying, 'That is not what we are hearing on the intercoms.'

The other useful trick is to invent stories to illustrate a point. This usually begins, 'I met a man today . . .' Again, no one can say you didn't meet him. You might have met him in the toilet when there was no one else around. You can invent anyone. You could tell a nursery rhyme this way and no one would notice:

'I met a man today . . . on his way to the fair. I asked him, "What do you have there?" He said, "Pies . . ." That's the kind of entrepreneurship we need in this country – just a simple pieman on his way to the fair.'

'I met a woman today, an old woman, and – this will illustrate the crisis in housing in this country – she was living in a SHOE. To make matters worse, she had so many children . . . Well, she was at her wits' end.'

'Just before I was going, a little girl came up to me, crying. She'd obviously been running and told me a story of how she was just going about her business, eating her curds and whey, when a spider – who, I might add, was out on bail – brutally accosted her and scared her away. The people of Ireland are living in FEAR.'

WHAT POLITICIANS ARE REALLY HEARING ON THE DOORSTEPS

I heard the doorbell,
Then nothing.
I thought there was
no one home.
Then I heard the
telly.
But the doorbell sounded
very positive.

Important figures

The election also marks the transition from the hypothetical to the actual – from people and ideas and feelings to NUMBERS.

A new shift of people will take over on the media to cut through the Bx. Called upon in our greatest hour of need, they turn up at election time and then afterwards they disappear. They are the electoral science experts – the psephologists. Like The Wolf, the Harvey Keitel character in *Pulp Fiction* who helps to get rid of a body, they turn up to do a job that no one else can do. Small talk mightn't be their strong suit. There are numbers to be worked. While the rest of us deal in emotion and gut instinct, these experts in 'pseph' could calculate a quota by the smell off the ballot box. They'd tell you what the swing was since the last election, taking into account constituency boundary changes, while you were still trying to find the start of a roll of Sellotape.

They know that all life and human existence and notions and pretensions are transitory and that numbers conquer all. You might think you're a special snowflake of a voter with your child called after a hero of the Fianna, a Bugaboo pram and a career in The Internet Of Things; however, you're nothing but a number, behaving on average exactly the same way as a Longford farmer in the general election of 1954, wondering whether to take a chance on Clann na Talmhan.

The people have spoken

And while we're cutting through the Bx, at the end of the election, there comes a rare time when some politicians finally let down their guard: the day of the count. There is no talk of policy or macho phrases like 'let's get real'. It's all about hard cold numbers. There is no more about what we are hearing on the doorsteps. The doorsteps have either spoken their mind or forgotten the date of the election.

The TD who doesn't get re-elected is finally able to talk about the lack of support from the party, the blunders the leader made, the dark hints about a party rival stealing posters and using them to put under the dogs on the puppy farm.

If you spend five years between elections frustrated by media interviews with politicians, you might as well make time to watch that one occasion when they'll speak their mind, when the mists of Media Training and Spin are lifted and you get to see the Tír na nÓg of what's on their mind. The politician may be in civvies – which is slightly unnerving, like seeing your teacher in jeans on sports day. The perfect moment has not yet happened, however. When a TD fails to retain their seat, the TV interviewer – and this is the height of bolloxology – under the guise of empathy, will continually press the candidate for reasons as to why the electorate turned against them:

And can you put the finger on why you lost and how do you feel now?

POLITICIAN *[losing it]*:
I lost. What more do ye want? What is this, *Liveline*? I'm going out for pints and f*ck ye all.

Of course, the winners can be just as easily exposed emotionally. Look at the faces of those newly elected TDs as they are hoisted high on the shoulders of supporters. There's elation there, naturally, but if you look closely enough you can detect a trace of terror in their faces as they are reminded of that birthday party when they were ten, when they were given the bumps and some 'friend' let them fall by mistake.

The Hames

Despite a dysfunctional political system, the country does function. But when it goes wrong, it goes very, very wrong. Hames were originally the pair of curved supports attached to the collar of a draft horse to which the traces were connected. Obviously, if these supports failed, the cart-pulling situation would degenerate into an awful hames. But it's more than a mess. It's a mess that could have been avoided had there been even the slightest bit of planning. It's a mess that often occurs at the end of a large, publicly funded endeavour, an endeavour that was launched three years previously with much fanfare but somewhere along the way, plan and practicality diverged and now there's an Official Inquiry and a lot of headed notepaper that will have to be thrown out after the name-change.

We can all make a hames of something. It's as human as catching the loop of the belt of your trousers on a door handle but when many humans with their belt-loop stuck in the door handle of life are handed large amounts of money then you get the omni-hames – the kind of situation where hundreds, even thousands of items of machinery that were supposed to herald a new way of measuring things are being stored in a warehouse somewhere in the midlands before eventually being sold for scrap.

The creation of a hames is governed by the following equation where N = Notions and H_{PU} = A Pure Hames:

$$N + B_X = H_{PU}$$

Here are the key steps in a hames:

• Something needs to be done. This is something. Do this.

• Get consultants in. Any type at all. Just get them in. If it goes wrong, blame them. But don't name them, obviously.

• Make a nice logo.

- Appoint someone who has a history of being involved in hameses to run it all.

- Launch the thing with a sod-turning exercise. This is to symbolize that we're the poor sods who'll have to pay for it.

- When it starts to go wrong, commission a report.

- Don't read the report. Press ahead.

- When it starts to go really wrong, use the report as a basis for an inquiry.

- Make sure the inquiry has no teeth.

- The minister in charge gets sent somewhere nice like the Seanad or Europe. Europe is the place politicians go at the end of it all. It's a bit like the end of *Lord of the Rings*. Having fought the big battle, they head to Valinor – the undying lands to the west (or the east in this case) – for a pension.

Let me take this opportunity to state that this book is campaigning for the hames to be given official recognition as a status – a bit like when the US President declares a Federal Disaster. So when a hames is declared, the following should happen:

• EVERYONE JUST STOP A MINUTE AND HAVE A LOOK AT THIS THING BEFORE WE GO ANY FURTHER.

• Call Batman.

10

Like No One's
Business

Jargon Outta That

Because 'it's all done on computers nowadays' and computer-speak has a habit of taking words that used to mean one thing and now mean another, like 'breadcrumbs' and 'cookies', business language changes fast.

It's as changeable as the language of teenagers, trends and what's 'cool'*. Business language often changes in order to get you to feel some semblance of excitement at doing whatever it was you were doing before.

*Of course, using the word 'cool' is as old fashioned as polishing your monocle or using your baby-finger to represent the receiver in miming 'call me'.

Reach out

This is an American import. It's hard to know where it came from but let it be said here now – it is utter bolloxology. Picture The Four Tops, three of them clicking fingers, swaying from side to side and lead singer Levi Stubbs building up to the almost semi-operatic climax of 'Reach Out (I'll Be There)'. And the other Tops join in at the emotional peak of the song. And why are they reaching out? Because their love will shelter you, naturally.

Now, imagine that you are being asked to reach out to Linda in Marketing because she has the most up-to-date version of the PowerPoint slides for Tuesday's Steering Group meeting. You are not reaching out to Linda. Linda works with you and this is part of both your jobs. She is not your last chance to stop your life from spiralling out of control or to keep the black dog of depression at bay. She just has some slides.

You need to stop reaching out. Just send people an email or ring them or talk to them. Save the reaching out for those whose love can shelter you.

Lookit, language is malleable and all that, but sometimes enough is enough. We've taken in enough awesomes and amazeballs and their ilk over the years. 'Reach out' is a bridge too far.

Key learnings

It's part of a creeping trend to use nouns as verbs and verbs as nouns. Some footballers have been known to 'goal with a few minutes to go to half-time.' The Olympics has brought us 'to medal' instead of 'to win a medal'. This means that if you were a champion philanderer, you could theoretically be said to medal in your own affairs.

Often, these verb–noun switches are done in order to soften the blow of other more straightforward words. Imagine you are in the office. Everyone is under pressure to get the Horizon 2030 project 'actioned' but there has been some 'scope creep'. In order to drive this project to meeting its KPIs, extra hours are going to be required – but how are you going to be persuaded to use up your spare bandwidth? Only if the manager emails you with 'an ask'.

A request is harsh. An ask is more friendly – although ultimately passive-aggressive. An ask says 'Hey, buddy, I'm as annoyed about this as you are but whaddyasay, sport? For the team?' An extension of this is the 'big ask'. If somebody says 'I know it's a big ask but . . .', then you know your weekend is gone.

Similarly, picture yourself at a conference. It's sometime in the torpor of the afternoon. Your body is telling you that it can't digest this chicken supreme with white sauce, baby potatoes and baton carrots AND watch a PowerPoint presentation where the font is too small.

If there's any hope at all of retaining anything from this day, it will have to be presented as a 'bunch of learnings' rather than lessons. The last thing the brain needs now is a lesson, which smacks too much of school and endless homework. A learning – especially a key

177

learning – is more gentle. The window is open. Everyone is dressed in white. Someone is holding your head and chanting.

The question that all pedants should ask themselves is precisely how angry one should get about all of this verb–noun switching. Is mild irritation sufficient or would spitting rage, banging doors and cancelling family excursions be an acceptable response? Is it time to execute an executive?

The answer is: be careful. Many of these switcheroos (sorry) and other jarring usages are older than you. 'Learnings' was used by Shakespeare. 'Ask' as a noun dates back a thousand years. Even 'presently' is presently OK. Your high moral ground may be a little eroded by time. Still though, 'key learnings'? Stop it.

The short goodbye

Talking about email is a waste of time because it will be replaced in a few years by something else – emoticons that you can produce by flicking a nostril at a heat-sensor in your iHand, perhaps. But for the time being, there is still a need to write electronic letters to people.

Beginning an email is relatively straightforward – you can employ a 'Hello/Howya/Howsitgoing' or, if you're down the country, 'Wellwhasdacraic'. There are still a few classy people who will open an email with 'Dear'. These people are to be cherished. The presence of 'Dear' makes the recipient of the email feel like they have been addressed by someone writing from a stately home, a fun-loving though disgraced earl confined to his bed, who will bequeath you a conundrum in his will.

But how should we end an email now? In school, we were all taught 'Yours faithfully' (when writing a letter of application for a bookkeeping role in an imaginary company) and 'Yours sincerely' (when writing to an imaginary penpal to invite them to camp on your uncle's farm and lying to them about the amenities in your area. 'But if it is raining we can *regarder la télévision.*')

Speaking of which, email has led to a surge in regards. People have once more taken to sending 'fond regards', 'kind regards', 'best regards'. 'The regard boom probably also led to the word 'irregardless', a word whose sole meaning is 'I'm not aware that irregardless is not a word'.

As well as 'best regards' there are 'best wishes', 'all the bests' and – the ultimate abbreviation – 'best'. Best what? Best-before date? Best not speak about this any more? Best get home and get the kettle on, Mrs Sugden?

'Best' has the effect of letting you know that actually you are, at best, getting their second-best or third-best regards because they're too busy to be writing regards to everyone.

Across this

'Yeah, I don't know what the mix-up was with your arrangements. I wasn't really across this during the week.'

Not being 'across it' sounds so much better than 'not doing my job'. 'Across' indicates a tycoon, their personality and drive spreading far beyond their physical presence. The fact they weren't aware of your problem is actually an indictment of how insignificant your problem is. But don't be fobbed off. Use the Crossword Clue Rule: if they weren't *across* it, then it must be *down* to them.

Disruption

'Disruption' is synonymous with air-traffic controllers in France and pupils who used to be 'bold'. But they'll have to find new names for those things because disruption has gone all computer. When the Minister for Innovatey Things talks about disruption more than the Minister for Strikes does, you know it's the bee's knees now. Or it was five minutes ago. It could have been disrupted again since I wrote this.

It's a fancy word for big change. If you've got a two-word company title, a three-word mission statement (see page 188) and there's a fussball table in the office, which you don't have time to play because you guys are just CANING it right now in time for the release of the beta version of upSkibble, an app that's going to blow Snakes and Ladders out of the water, chances are you're in the disruption game.

Traditional industries are being eviscerated by seventeen-year-old coders who, by rights, should be out in the park, drinking cans like we did at that age, but who fell in with no crowd and are now CEOs. Impossibly precocious '30 to Watch Under 30'-somethings who are lauded by politicians at the opening of AnotherCon, a meeting of some of the industry's top minds to discuss the end of history and the start of the future.

You too can be part of the disruption. Just take any aspect of normal everyday life: what would happen if we burnt it and started again with something that you could do from your phone? Here are a few possibilities we just whiteboarded while the kettle was boiling:

- **Your father's tablets.** Is your father always forgetting to take his tablets? That represents 'latent tablet potential' that could be freed up on the open market. There are *always* people looking for tablets. Siphon off some of them – the health system will keep handing them over anyway, in lieu of care – and set up drug*PRESS*, a sharing economy, peer-to-peer marketplace where the squeezed middle can unlock the potential of their parents' medicine cabinets.

- **The bins.** Turns out some of us have been disrupting the whole bin-collection industry already by dumping our waste next to municipal bins or areas of outstanding natural beauty. But maybe it's time a tremendous source of human capital was harnessed by a bright young graduate and the lads from his final-year project. Introducing shnakeyBin – an app that allows you to have your bins emptied and dumped in a skip two doors down. You just put in your location, the address of a neighbour who seems far too pleased with himself and shnakeyBin does the rest.

- **imoHooRim.** The modern world needs your opinion but you may not have time to do the requisite reading. imoHooRim comes from an Irish phrase, meaning 'In my opinion (which I wasn't asked for and no one is interested in)'. It allows you to outsource all your opinion-forming by scouring the comments made by your social network friends. It will generate opinions, which may not have any basis in fact, for you on a variety of topics. If you pay for the premium service, it will actually post those opinions for you as comments, thus freeing up valuable time for you to see if anyone has given you likes.

- **toolkIT.** Disrupting networking. How do you know who to avoid at social gatherings? toolkIT helps you spot the tools in any group. It uses facial recognition to scan people's social network accounts and tell you exactly what they're like. For example, if their LinkedIn profile mentions that they are 'passionate about delivering excellence in the cloudspace', then you know they're probably a great goy and all that but perhaps a bit of a knob. If, on the other hand, their Facebook page is filled with enigmatic photos of *actual* clouds and accompanied by a Native American quote or something about angels written in a handwritey typeface, then you can assume that they're harmless enough but you wouldn't want to get stuck talking to them.

If you can't beat them, create synergies with them

There's no point getting upset about office jargon; you can put up with it, complain about it, or do something about it. Whatever you do, you'll either need to mothball it or escalate it.

Jargon has its place but as words become overused, they grow stale and meaningless. As 'dynamic', 'engage', 'drive growth' and 'unlock your company's potential' lose their potency, why not create your own?

Too much of the existing jargon annoys people because it has no resonance for them. Take 'blue-sky thinking' – you could be waiting weeks for a blue sky in this country. 'Thinking outside the box'? How can you think outside of the box if you don't know where the edges of the box are? 'Low-hanging fruit'? You can't pick fruit yourself now because of insurance and anyway it's so cheap to just get it on special in Lidl.

We should root new jargon in real experience. Like domestic life:

- **Let's see if there are any woodlice under the mat.** No one sweeps anything under the carpet any more. It's all wooden floors. But somewhere in every house there is a mat with woodlice under it.

- **This is a real teabag-left-in-the-sink moment.** What are the trivial issues on the project that could have a disproportionate effect on perception and relationships?

- **Who's going to be our extension lead on this one? And does he have enough flex?** There isn't a person in the country who hasn't at some point wished for more plug sockets. But if we do get someone in with multiple skills, will they still be so attached to the old way of doing things that they will effectively be useless?

- **Have we dusted the skirting-boards**? Is every detail taken care of? Even the less obvious ones?

- **Throw the clothes on the floor**. The deadline is approaching. We don't have time to put away all the underpants and socks that are currently on the project duvet. Just horse the whole lot on to the floor and we'll put them away in the morning.

Farming can be another rich source of new metaphors. Farming is the new tech. With this little country aiming to feed the world with milk products, we are headed for a Milk Boom – the Celtic Udder. Instead of Silicon Valley, the Golden Vale will be Milk-can Valley. Irish farmers could become flush. For years, they swore to the taxman and/or anyone who'd listen that they didn't have so much as a ten-bob note to spare. Now will we see Milk Sheikhs with their gold-plated Almeras and Passats lined up outside the mart? Hip-hop stars will be attracted to the scene. Crews with names such as NWA (Nitrates With Attitude), the Beastings Boys and the Notorious Ciba-Geigy will lead the way.

And just like tech, farming metaphors could make the cross-over into business speech. Farming metaphors have been used in office jargon for donkey's years. People have 'taken the bull by the horns', 'ploughed their own furrow' and 'brought home the bacon' for a long time. There is potential for many more.

- **Who'll make hay on this?** Who'll take the risk on hay rather than taking the easy option and making silage? Who is willing to put in the work to cut, turn, cock or bale something instead of just baling and wrapping it?

- **Have we tried to get the site off the father?** Sometimes the simplest solution is staring you in the face. Maybe you've had a row with the father and are not speaking but now is the time to sweat the existing assets. If the stubborn oul eejit would only listen for a minute.

- **You can't dose the cattle if they're not in the crush.** This is a saying explicitly designed to avoid a hames (see page 170). A bit like getting your ducks in a row, don't proceed to the next stage of a project without waiting until each earlier step is done.

- **I think we need to wait for the AI man on this one.** There is a seminal moment in every project where a good programme manager realizes that it's time to bring in an outside expert. Bringing the bull to the cow is a nice option to have (or nice to be had) but at the end of the day sometimes the black box – or syringe – is what's required.

- **Who's 'bush-gapping' this project?** Who's looking ahead on the project's critical path to make sure there aren't any places the project's cattle could run into and make ribbons of the project's neighbour's garden? Because the project would never hear the end of it from that fella and he might sue the project like he threatened to do the time his polytunnel was destroyed.

Inundated with Innovation

Everything is innovative now. Companies are constantly finding new ways of doing things instead of just leaving the bloody thing alone. Most innovation happens not because we need A Better Thing but because the company that makes the Thing wants us to buy a new one even though the one we have is grand. People who only need the computer for the email and to do a newsletter for the Tidy Towns are being urged to 'upgrade to unlock the full power of Windows 10' even though the laptop can barely play YouTube, and even then only in the box room, for some reason.

Naming your business

Naming your company with 'tech' or 'solutions' at the end is *soooo* 2000s. You need to twoWORD it. The two words don't need to be swanky words themselves. In fact, the more ordinary the constituent parts, the more it highlights how innovative the whole thing is. Companies like trouserBISCUIT, spadeCRAYON and carpetHANDLE don't exist yet but, mark myWORD, they soon will.

What this will say is that your business is 'changing the way the world looks at drainpipes for ever'.

(Innovative naming in the craft-y and hospitality industries is different. Bars and restaurants now need to evoke a time when there was attention to detail, when everyone had a moustache and ran whittling workshops, watched by their children who were learning the time-honoured tradition.

That's why you will see a lot of new companies with names that resemble characters in lesser-known Dickens or Twain novels. Enjoy a whiskey at Collywinkle and Sturgible. Pay eight euro for sliced pan at Gunther Solversson's Minnesota Trading Outpost.)

Three little words

If you're innovative about what you do, you'll need to explain it all to idiots like the rest of us. That's where the three-word mission statement comes in. Pick any three words that sound good even on their own. Separate them using full stops. Stick them at the top of your website. Bob's. Your. Uncle. Their function is to make your customers feel like more than an invoice. They are part of an experience, a movement. Classic ones include: 'Create. Enjoy. Live.' Or 'Work. Be. Know.'

But don't be limited by this. Combine any three words, put them in a nice typeface and the Bx will flow.

Innovate. Create. Prostrate.

Plough. Harrow. Slurry.

Do. Gwan. AhDo.

But it's not just for the new companies. There's been enough adoration of innovation; it's time to celebrate maintenance. We should be promoting Ireland as a Centre of Maintenance. Send diplomats to trade shows with pull-up banners bearing slogans such as:

Ireland – Who Put That In For You?
A Bit of a Cowboy Effort, I'd Say.

And to give the maintainers their due, they should have some of the bolloxological glory. For any 'maintrepreneurs', here's your three-word path to wealth:

mendIT: Shrug. Sigh. Fix.

Work–Love Balance

Passion and inspiration – they're everywhere now. They're positive words but ripe for bolloxology.

We may have reached peak passion. A careers advice ad earlier this year began: 'Are you passionate about accounting?' Now, don't get me wrong. It's perfectly plausible that accounting might evoke strong feelings. Anyone who has ever done Business Studies in school will remember how pleasure and pain were on two sides of a skinny coin when it came to adding up that thing where you were supposed to get the same answer in the left column and the right column. If you got it right, joy was unconfined. If you got it wrong, you sank further into your chair as the miasma of steaming coats on the too-hot radiator seeped into your addled brain during the Long Dark Afternoon Double-class of the Soul.

This is not to diss the noble profession of accountancy. It's a worthy skill. It separates those with knowledge from the spoofers. Like techies, accountants have a confidence about them that says, 'I'd have the solutions sketched out on the back of an envelope in the time it would take you to find a pen that works'. It's just hard to believe that even people who like accounting are *passionate* about it. Or that they should be. You could argue we got into the last property crash because people were a little too passionate in their accounting.

There's no blame on the people who designed the ad. Hyperbole-inflation has devalued lots of words already. A 'legend' used to be someone who fought multiple-headed monsters with an enchanted sword. Now it's just some lad fighting multiple guards outside a takeaway. Epic.

So it is with 'passionate'. Once one person told LinkedIn they were passionate about their job, now we all have to be. Anything less than this heat of intense feeling towards whatever it is you are doing – be it social media manager or office administrator or mildly contrarian author – implies you are lukewarm about it.

In a competitive job market, you can't just show enthusiasm, it has to be an 'enthusi-gasm'. Job interviews now need to distinguish the one-night stands from those who will keep the spark alive for years.

'So, you say you are an expert in cloud computing . . . but would you describe yourself as passionate and evangelical about it? I need to know you'd be willing to go to jail for it or take a bullet. Anyone can love their job but I'm looking for someone *in love*.'

As a result, judging from people's social media bios, job adverts and CVs, such a large proportion of our workforce are passionate about what they do, it's a wonder the nation's offices, building sites and retail outlets aren't heaving with bodies writhing between the time sheets. As the bedsprings of the workplace creak with all that passion, the rest of us have the nagging fear that our dry, passionless existence means we may never achieve our full potential. But don't worry about fulfilling your potential. It's best to leave a bit of potential unfulfilled for the time being – like hiding toilet roll under the sink and then forgetting about it. Or the emergency fiver in the car.

The explosion in 'passion' can be traced to the self-improvement industry. It encourages us all to *pursue* our hopes and dreams. So, if can say you're passionate about what you do – be it stacking pallets or shaping customer-activation strategy to drive success going forward – then clearly you have been successful in your pursuit and caught up with your passion.

It all sounds quite emotionally draining. And if you're drained, you might need a pep-talk . . .

I don't think you're passionate enough about your work!

But I am...

You need to prove your love for the job!

I will!

BZZZ

INKLING™
4 ALL UR
PRINTER
INK
NEEDS

Oul Talks

We are in a boom time for talks. A speech can feel too dogmatic; it implies that you are talking *at* people. Instead you can give a Talk.

And anyone can give a Talk. Picture the scene.

There is a ripple of applause, the kind of applause they have in America with their politeness and big rooms. You're alone on the stage. It's pitch black all around you but you are perfectly lit, with a large screen above your head, a clicker in your hand and one of those mics that you'd hardly know was there.

You're giving a TED talk.

If you think 'hearing a talk' means going to the parish hall to hear a local historian – a man with a shed full of books on place names and forty-year-old copies of the *Tuam Herald* – or getting advice in Transition Year on careers or cyberbullying, then think again. Talk used to be cheap but now it's premium. TED talks and others like it are big business.

TED stands for Technology Entertainment Design. It's a great concept and a lot of TED talkers are high achievers with fascinating, powerful and affecting viewpoints.

Luckily for any aspiring bolloxologists, there is plenty of room as well for shite-talk. So if you fancy a rapt audience, it's time for some TEDbxTalks. You just need to follow a few basic rules.

Your name

You need a good name. While Gerry Carrigan, Donie Welch and Niamh Halligan are beautiful names, if you're going to stand in an auditorium (not a hall; this isn't a table quiz) and enlighten, you need a better one.

You need a name that implies a certain power. It should tell a story in itself: you're from America or your parents were diplomats and you went to one of those international schools where they don't spend any time doing Irish or Religion but instead study The World. You need to imply that you've been to Geneva, not because you've a brother there but because you've business there.

So, pick a name like Max Guilders, Beanie Jones, Orlando Samosa, Carson Beauchamp, Joaquin Strode, Sterling Rosenbloom, Shannon Shoe, Benicio Sands, Pippie Hauser, Thursday Eastwood, Skate Montalban, Lauren Pagliagli-Connor, Faith Ngoh or Skyler Stewart.

Appearance

Next, you need to dress the part. If you're a man, wear dark-coloured jeans, a lighter coloured blazer and open-necked shirt. If you're a woman, go for a sober black trouser suit, perhaps accessorized by a colourful silk scarf but it shouldn't matter because the whole point of this talk is about how appearances can be deceiving.

Have some sort of achievement for your biog (but it doesn't have to have a point)

'In 2014 I became the first person to row barefoot backwards up the seven highest mountain streams of the world.' No one asked you to do it. It's doubtful what was achieved but this was Your Thing. You went and let the family hold down the fort so that you could do Your Thing. And that's part of the inspiration. Just fecking off.

Opening gambit

Now, on to the talk. Start with something simple like, 'Let me ask you a question'. You're immediately drawing in the audience, telling them this is not just a talk, but a conversation. This is for them. They, too, are important like you. Or could be, if they listen to you.

Handy questions could be:

- How long is a second?

- What do you think about when I ask 'Who are you?'

- Have you ever wondered how we have so much leisure but so little time?

You don't have to answer the question. People may think you've answered it but that they somehow missed it or are not clever enough to have got it. Or else you can return to it at the end and say: 'A second is as long you want it to be. You are who you decide to be. The answer to that lies inside each and every one of us.'

Quotes

Quotes are vital in any TEDbxTalk. Most normal people go through their lives not quoting anyone famous. They may quote their friends: 'Well she said now that he wasn't supposed to be up there at all but anyway didn't the squad car arrive and off with yer man to the Bridewell.' At best, most of us can quote 'the fella': 'As the fella said, it's better than a kick in the face from a cow protecting her calf.' But rarely do we quote anyone famous. Sometimes this is simply because we don't know if that famous person said it or not. We might have got a book of quotations once as a Christmas present but usually that's about it.

None of this matters in a TEDbxTalk. You can make up what you like and pretend someone famous once said it. If they're dead or far away, you can put any words into anyone's mouth.

> • ... and the Dalai Lama said, 'That's where I carried you.' 'But,' said the little boy, 'what about the bit where there's only one footprint in the sand?' 'That,' said the Dalai Lama, 'that was when you hopped.'

• Martin Luther King taught us that we are not alone when he said, 'You are not alone.'

• The great philosopher Deepak Chopra calls this the 'pain-in-the-hole' conundrum.

• And the man in the carriage ... was Albert Einstein.

You could also throw in one jokey one that shows you are in touch with popular culture but only in a slightly patronizing way and then go on to make a serious point about boundaries:

• I like to quote one of the great thinkers of our time, Snoop Doggy Dogg *[wait for snickers from the audience who've heard of him, or if they haven't, think the name sounds funny]* and his song 'Gin And Juice' *[and then find a line which coincidentally sounds like it fits your talk about Reimagining Tomorrow, when in fact SDD was talking about smoking a blunt with his homies]*.

• But seriously ... we have a lot to learn from Mattress Mick when he said, 'You can't have a good day with a bad mattress and you can't have a bad day with a good mattress. . .'

The problem with the modern world

The problem with the modern world as you articulate it in one of these talks is that we were promised so much but it didn't happen; we think we're happy but we're not. Stick to this formula and you can't go wrong, as these examples show:

- We are so busy in our lives that we aren't even aware that the dust gathering around us is made up of tiny bits of us, flaking away to nothing.

- The paradox of our time is that the more stuff we buy, the more stuff we have to put under the stairs behind the hoover.

- We build bigger and bigger houses to accommodate all the stuff we buy but at the same time the space in our hearts gets smaller because we've stored some of the stuff in there.

- We can do so much in two minutes. We can travel to the moon. We can give birth to a child. We can chop down a tree.

- Can you afford to? Can you afford *not* to? (Just have this line with no context.)

- The present becomes the past, like, really quickly. That sentence is already in the past. So is that one.

But the *future* is always in the future until it briefly becomes the present and then goes into the past. The question is – what tense are you living in? Is it past tense or . . . JUST TENSE?

• Look into your heart for the inspiration and the actions will follow just like night follows day, like cats follow fatally wounded birds.

Connect two things that are not related

It's your talk, so the audience will assume you know everything.

'Have you ever found it perplexing that we have travelled all the way to the moon and back but we struggle to start a conversation across the road or across the train carriage?'

Don't worry that those are two completely different things. One is a decades-long project involving collaboration between thousands of engineers and the other is just two people who don't need to talk to each other unless one wants to have a look at the other's paper on the train and then she'll ask because that's how Mammy operates.

'Why is it that we can hold a baby gently in our arms but at the same time destroy a forest?'

Because it's my child and I didn't destroy the forest.

'What is strange about the modern age is that we can have enough to eat but at the same time have a hunger in our hearts.'

Again, this is not a strange thing at all. It's called life. Come to think, that's a great title for a TEDbxTalk: 'It's Called Life.'

11

Get With the
Programmes

WE ARE IN A GOLDEN AGE of television. Every
bloody series is a must-watch. This has left us more
unsettled than ever. We're either under pressure to
get all our TV tasks done, or we're dying to get on the
telly. No one is afraid of the spotlight any more. People
used to freeze on the £5 question on *Murphy's Micro
Quiz-M*. Now children are calmly coining phrases about
tractors or reciting poems about dead ponies on the
Late Late Toy Show.

Spoiler Alert

'Hold on a second – how far are you into it?' As a
question, out of context, it doesn't seem to make much
sense. Perhaps if your friend was lost in a maze and
rang you from inside it because they knew you'd already

made your way out of it and therefore could guide them through it, then you would have cause to say it.

But many of us repeat this phrase quite often in social gatherings. It's necessary because we need to avoid that thing that has the potential to ruin an evening as surely as a bout of food poisoning: the spoiler.

If you think spoilers are just aerodynamic structures made of lightweight polymers and fixed to the front or back of a Subaru driven at 7,000 revs from the Spar to the Cineplex so that its growl can be heard across the landscape like a lion in heat on the Serengeti, then, spoiler alert: they are so much more than that.

The spoiler is that tiny phrase uttered by someone who has finished the book, seen the match, is further along in the box set than you, and which renders all your future experience of the match, book or TV show moot.

It used to be that the spoiler was largely concerned with football matches. You would tiptoe through the day, avoiding human contact, so that you could watch *Match of the Day* or *The Sunday Game* with no idea what the result was.

Now, spoilers permeate every conversation. And if you haven't seen the programme everyone's talking about, conversations can become kind of awkward because the other person is DYING to talk about something but can't because you haven't been enlightened. They can't enlighten you. They can only encourage you to access it for yourself via a computer programme. It's like talking to a cagey Scientologist.

'So, how far are you in?'

'I've only seen a couple of episodes.'

'Ah, so you haven't got as far as the bit where . . . Oh. I shouldn't say.'

'Is it bad?'

'No, no, it's just . . . not what you'd expect.'

'Any hints? Without giving anything away?'

'Well . . . you know the way Elderthon Sagworth died in the first episode?'

'WHAT?! Elderthon's DEAD?!'

'Oh crap – I thought you said you'd seen the first couple of episodes! Wait, which season did you mean?'

'There's more than one?'

'Oh my God, yeah, we're up to season five now!'

'Oh no, I can't believe Elderthon's gone! He was the best thing in the show. What happened to him?'

'He was killed by Toolsbane Halfwilly.'

'Who's he?'

'Skon Dukesfilter's son.'

'Skon has a son?! But I thought he was dead!'

'No, he was brought back to life.'

'Look, I think you'd better go.'

Even if you do avoid the spoilers and start watching a series, your happiness is going to be short-lived. It means that other series will be pushed further back in the queue. You'll have a *backlog* of telly, which is more onerous than any never-ending TO-DO list. And just like the aspirational TO-DO lists in work notebooks, we are coming to the sad conclusion that there might just be too much television to finish in our natural lifetimes. We may have to compile a list for future generations. You don't have time for that so you watch the first few episodes in a state of tension, waiting for it to get good. You ask your friends' advice. One tells you to 'stick with it'. Another says 'ten hours of my life I won't get back.' Aaaaagh. Once again the bolloxology of the modern world is the tyranny of choice.

Beginning a series now makes you feel like your biological clock is ticking. You have an imaginary conversation with the TV show, much as you would with a prospective partner in one of those upfront conversations early on in the relationship. You need to know if this programme is The One.

'Are you any good? You'd better be good because I don't have time to waste on you if you turn out to be a by-the-numbers police procedural, like all the others.'

Just like in a relationship, this can put too much of a strain on the early episodes of the show and often, unless there's a twist, such as the hero being killed early on, you and the TV show sadly go your separate ways.

Do you remember when there was nothing on? Those wet summer evenings when the only backlog was one of scattered showers and you wrung every last minute of sustenance out of the two channels with their TV shows that wouldn't even pass muster now. *Jake and the Fatman* didn't have a brooding anti-hero, women being targeted by a serial killer who delighted in prime-number puzzles, or a troubled cop whose biggest adversary *is inside his own head*. Still, we watched the marrow out of it on bored evenings when regular television was on holidays.

Our minds were lean. We only got steak once a week with something like *Robin of Sherwood* (the mystical one with Michael Praed). Now, we're all obese, with our recommended weekly requirement of good telly exceeded by Monday night.

And we're permanently on a state of alert for spoilers.

Spoilers are so feared now they've permeated the real world too. One day you'll meet a friend you haven't seen in ages. Before filling them in on the intervening years, you'll hesitate. Should you tell him all that has happened in sequential order? What happens if you spoil the series? Best to start with: 'Hold on a second. My life: I'm in season thirty-eight now . . . where are you in it?'

WHAT THEY SAY

Are you watching
<TV SHOW>?

You should!
you'd like
it.

No?

WHAT THEY MEAN

Are you watching
<TV SHOW>?

You should,
because
I've no one
to talk to
about it.

No, I've too
many shows to
watch already.

Reality Check

We Irish can laugh at ourselves, according to the old saying. To be more accurate, we Irish get a bit awkward seeing ourselves on television because it reminds us of what we are like, so we tend to lash out.

And let's face it, there's a lot of us to see on television now. Almost every human activity has been rendered into a competitive TV show.

It's easy for the rest of us to sneer at *Ireland's Fittest Family*. By 'the rest of us', I mean Ireland's Average-est, Not That Bothered-est, and I've Enough To Be Doing Keeping Ye In Phone Credit-est Families.

Hearing the stars of these shows talk about how they exercise and work out together is designed to bring on a warm fuzzy feeling as we reflect on how nice it is for a family to share the same interest. Of course, we don't know if every member is included. There could be a Goth child off-camera, sighing about how no one understands him. By and large, though, the families seem well-adjusted, with low body fat.

There's nothing wrong with shows about acts of physical endurance. It's just the bit where they have to put the experience into words. The premise of most of these shows is: Do the hard thing in the shortest period of time. But because there's half an hour to fill and the tasks are repetitive, we have to listen to ordinary people speak fluent sportish with surreal references thrown in:

'Yeah, we knew if we were fully focused, giving it 110 per cent, with our shoulder to the wheel; that if we were in the lead coming up to the Bog Snorkel, we'd be in with a good shout. Credit to the lads, at the end of the day we'll just have to see if our Rope of Death was good enough. To be fair.'

By current estimates, a quarter of all human free time in Ireland is spent watching other people competitively cook, bake, renovate, decorate or lose weight. We're really waiting for someone to have a meltdown, throw the whole lot in the bin/skip and go out and have a fag. It doesn't happen often enough. Architects preside over marital difficulties like a counsellor who hopes to patch over a relationship's flaws with a nice bit of fascia or open up the whole space to the light.

With so many activities now 'realitized', it's only a matter of time before everything else is converted into TV gold. Here are a few early contenders:

- *Ireland's Best Chuggers*. The cameras follow the shiniest-faced, most optimistic charity workers as they compete to sign up the greatest number of old ladies for direct debits to puppy charities for the rest of their lives.

- *Dishwasher-Off*. Families are presented with two days' washing-up and they have to fit it all in the dishwasher. The challenge comes from the fact that every family has to work with a stranger who may have a completely different stacking-philosophy. Or even worse, they may be the slovenliest student ever to be spoiled by a mother, who'll put the Waterford Crystal in with the lasagne dish. A special celebrity charity version called *Rinse-Aid* will be broadcast at Christmas.

• ***Ireland's Fittest Fitters***. Watch as the contestants compete to install as many gas boilers in a day as possible. The boilers are all in the wrong place (WHOEVER BUILT THIS HOUSE SHOULD BE SHOT) and all the jobs are in city-centre locations so they have to either park half a mile away or illegally and finish the job before they are clamped.

• ***Ireland's Clampiest Clampers***. A spin-off of the above. Other variations include *Water Meter Installers v. Protesters*.

• ***Broadband Wars***. Family members compete against each other to find the best broadband reception in the house. Bonus points are given if you manage to BitTorrent a whole series of *Breaking Bad*.

• ***Ireland's Best Old Couple***. Instead of a crass dating show with giggling callow youths, we put couples who've been together forty years through their paces in a series of trials including Those Underpants Could Do With A Wash, How Can We

Get Out Of Going To That Wedding, Changing Our Prescriptions and Figuring Out The New Bypass. (There would be huge demand for this. As the TV shows *Gogglebox* and, especially, *First Dates* have shown, old couples are far more interesting. While the younger people are staring anywhere but at their date or nipping to the toilet to ring a friend to say 'Omigod, Shaz, he's so weird', the old couple take us back to a different, bygone era of romantic interaction. It's like all those films where Anthony Hopkins spends decades trying to convey his fondness for a lady by gently adjusting his spectacles on his nose and furiously polishing a spoon. But with an Irish twist where they make jokes about how 'all their bits are still in working order'.)

• *Ireland's Handiest TDs.* The TDs are set a series of tasks like Getting A Stairlift Put In For Your Mam and Writing To The Minister About That One. They are voted out at the end of each episode but the voting is often the best bit. RTÉ would love it because it's done with the single transferable vote so the programme could go on for a week, with tallymen brought in to lean on railings.

• *Ireland's Best Funerals.* Scheduling for this would be a bit tricky but the premise is finding out which contestant gets the best send-off. They are judged on the quality of the sandwiches, the eulogy, how many TDs turned up, what kind of stories were told about them, laughing at the back of the church. After that, they are judged on the life they led by celebrity judge God.

• **Ireland's Next Top *Late Late Show* Guest.** The ultimate prize – an appearance on *The Late Late Show*, the adulation of everyone from the parish at home and abuse from everyone watching the show on Twitter. Contestants must compete in rounds such as The Heart-breaking Story, What Do You Think Of Irish Audiences? and Debate About The Big Issue With The Usual Latchikos That'd Be On The Panel.

How to Write an Ad for Irish Radio

In order to write virtually any advertisement in Ireland, you only need to know a few basic rules:

- If you're from the North, you like to help people with their depression or their food-poisoning concerns.

- If you're from Cork, you mainly worry about something being too expensive.

- All children are from Dundrum Shopping Centre and, get this – it turns out they know more than their parents about how to get good value on their utility bills. Who'd have known?

- Women like shopping and feel guilty about not spending enough time with their ageing mothers.

- If you've a working-class Dublin accent and you haven't established yourself as a reliable mechanic, chances are you're up to no good.

- Men are not able to fix the thing that's broken around the house but they'll still try.

- Every so often the client will want to feature in

the ad themselves. This will make it sound like the owner is acting under duress.

• Sports stars couldn't care less about the product they are endorsing. "'[Product] helps me achieve 110 per cent." Can I go now?'

Here are some scripts to get you started.

Scene
A rustling of paper
indicates a couple going
over the bills.

Husband:	What's wrong, darling? You seem upset.
Wife:	It's this middle-class problem I have. Something to do with a mortgage or a financial product.
Man with Dublin Accent:	I can help 'n all in anyways. Torremolinos, *Evenin' Herdald*, the gargle.
Middle-class Voiceover:	When you have a middle-class problem, don't try to cut corners and go to someone who talks like that man you just heard. He's

going to be quite short-termist in his outlook and all of his transactions will be largely cash-based. You need a Reassuring Middle-class Male like me.

Wife: Reassuring Middle-class Male?

Middle-class Voiceover: Yes, someone who talks like this will fix your problem, unless it's a mechanic you're looking for.

Man with Dublin Accent: I'm a mechanic 'n all in anyways. Well, I'm good at getting into a car, wha'!

Middle-class Voiceover: Don't mind him – he's on smack. You need Reassuring Working-class Dublin Male for Your Car. Let's call him My Good Man. Now he hasn't been to university, obviously. We can't all go. Someone has to fix the cars, haha. But he does have some very useful skills. You may even be able to have some banter with him when he arrives but, all the same, you would be disappointed if your daughter married him.

Man with **Dublin Accent:**	AH WHERE AM I TO GO TO IN ALL BU'H?

Burglar alarm sounds.

Middle-class **Voiceover:**	New alarm systems – keeping the working class out of YOUR home.

The other basic ad template revolves around the conflict in a home when a man tries to fix something that is beyond his skills. The woman then has to call someone professional to sort it out. This is despite having so many other things on her mind, like her guilt about not looking after her mother.

Scene
Sound of hammer banging
and background shouting.

Child:	Mum! What's Dad doing up on the roof?
Mum:	Oh! You know your father, what a tool! He's trying to fix the roof himself.
Child:	But why does he not get EXPERT EXPERTS to fix it?

Mum: I guess he's just insecure about the changing roles in society and the mixed messages he's been getting about what masculinity means now, but frankly I don't have time to worry about his insecurities. I need to know who's going to mind my mother.

Reassuring Middle-class Woman Voiceover: Wondering how to look after your mother can be a guilt-inducing feeling for all women. You really should do it yourself but you're so busy with the kids and there's no mention of the husband taking time off. OK, We'll Mind Your Mam So is a professional service that will ease your mind. And you're going to be hearing a lot more from us. Because for us, 'old is gold'.

BolloxFest

Bands You Know

BANDS YOU PRETEND TO KNOW WRITTEN

IN INCREASINGLY smaller FONTS

until you wonder if some are MADE UP.

· STAGES · THAT · ARE · NOT · MUSIC ·

· Comedy because you're too hungover for music.
· Some sort of Literary tent · Something else like whittling or facepainting · Some event where you are only there to hide from the rain ·

Artisan food
from a Very Fancy
burger van.
(or Ice cream van!)

Plastic Pints of Beer
from
whatever company
sponsors the festival
or the slab you brought!

Part Three

SOCIAL

12

Auntie Social

IT IS A MEASURE OF HOW important 'social' has become that it gets a whole section to itself in this book – perhaps the most important book published with this title, this week.

Like many other innovations, such as contraception or the wheel, social networking was treated with suspicion at the start. Mainstream media chortled at it. 'It's just people saying what they had for their dinner.' (This is ironic given that mainstream media devote a huge amount of time telling people what celebrity chefs are *about* to make for *their* dinners.)

But soon social networking became mainstream and now it's often just referred to as 'social'. So, in theory, you could work for a company on its 'social', make friends at a company social and then, if the company loses money and needs to *downsize*, you may end up on 'the social'.

Social networking, like private and public networking, is about creating a 'version' of yourself and that is a recipe for bolloxology of the highest order. ('Order of Bolloxology' is a figurative term. There is no Order of Bolloxology to be conferred by the Queen, but if she did it would be appended to a name as in 'Colm O'Regan OBx'.)

There are many different social networks on the go now. One reason for their proliferation is that teenagers are constantly fleeing adults from social network to social network, looking for a bit of privacy (from adults, not from each other). So a lot of teenagers will not join Facebook because their mothers and fathers are there already, putting up photos of them standing awkwardly at a family occasion.

So, while parents ruin Facebook with their 'Thoughts and prayers are with those in . . .' and 'Sorry for the rant, guys, but . . .', teenagers have moved to Instagram and Snapchat. And when parents arrive there, the youth will move on again to the next social network – such as HUH? (where you and friends can just sigh together) or OKAAAAAAY (a social network you can storm out of).

Uses for Facebook

Facebook is still the most-used network and even if you're not feeling particularly social-able you can just observe human nature through virtual people-watching. Here are the kinds of people you can meet.

The friends who accept a friend request from anyone

A brief flutter of excitement grips you. There's a notification! The magic, red '1' next to the two heads symbol at the top of your screen. It's a Facebook friend invite.

'That's an unusual name. How did they hear about me? Maybe I'm more famous than you thought. Let's see . . . Maria de Sousa Oliveira . . . what's your story? Oh, you seem to share a lot of advertisements for sunglasses and you have a link to your website which is . . . Oh, I see. Lots of pictures of you with very little on.'

You click on 'Ignore'.

'That was a lucky escape. But it says we have one mutual friend. Who's that? Oh, I see. The dirty divil.'

Despite all its faults, every so often Facebook gives you a tiny giggle as you see which respected civil rights campaigner/school principal/HR manager/nurse among your friends has been intrigued enough by a Brazilian adult-movie star to accept their friend request.

How to tell if Someone is a WEREDUCK!!

1. They have feathers on them!!

This is from my pillow!

2. They're mad for bread!

I love bread but it's so bad for me!

3. They have a duck's face in selfies!

Those who think life's problems can be solved using a morality tale about what's really important, deep down, you know, when you really think about it

A Facebook friend who normally shares nothing except the local shopping centre's 'Like and share for a chance to win a Renault Clio' offer has just posted a long piece of text. This could be interesting. Maybe they want to share something personal and you, you nosy fecker, are *dying* to see what they'll say. It usually begins with one of the following:

• A little boy asked his grandfather one day, 'Grandpa, what's a cow?!'

• A young girl looked at her father. The man had tears in his eyes . . .

• 'Son, I don't need a piece of paper to prove to you I'm from this country. The leg I lost in 'Nam should tell you all you want to know . . .'

Ah, forget it. It's one of those morality tales about the innocence of children, the wisdom of grandparents, the busyness of the modern world, our skewed priorities, how kids these days just got their noses stuck in these damn screens and can't in tarnation just look at a beautiful sunset. Or else it's a veteran soldier waving his medals in the face of some soft-handed-commie-liberal pen-pusher who works in the Veterans Benefits Office.

What your friend has shared on Facebook will damage your faith in humanity, which had been previously restored!

You obviously can't say anything to them, even though you're dying to. One of your loveliest friends, a person with a difficult university degree, a demanding career and who is doing a fine job raising a wonderful family, somehow thinks *this* is a good idea:

> 'As of 1 January, Facebook has updated its privacy notice. Everything you've ever posted becomes public from tomorrow. Even messages that have been deleted or the photos not allowed. It costs nothing for a simple copy and paste, better safe than sorry. Channel 13 News talked about the change in Facebook's privacy policy.'

C'mon, man. It was on Channel 13? And you only have Saorview? Channel 13 is Lyric FM. Didn't any of this strike you as suspicious?

This is one of myriad hoaxes that appear on Facebook all the time, warning you about something. For those of you who do not use Facebook: imagine that there is a community text-alert system in your area for telling people to watch out for strange vans in the area in case it's latchikos stealing lawnmowers. But instead of warning you about those, it warned you about non-existent latchikos and told you that you could protect yourself by putting a turnip on your doorstep. And you put the turnip on your doorstep and everyone knew you were an eejit. And it wouldn't stop the latchikos anyway because they were coming in the back window.

'I know some of you won't copy and paste this but. . .' I'll tell you why we won't copy and paste it. BECAUSE IT DOESN'T MAKE ANY DIFFERENCE SO STOP PASSIVE AGGRESSIVELY ROPING US INTO A POINTLESS EXERCISE.

And if you're going to copy and share any messages, make it this one:

> 'It's official, folks. I heard it on Channel 57 local news. From October 2016, the book *Bolloxology* is available in every bookshop. I know some of you won't do this but tell all your friends to buy copies of *Bolloxology*. If you don't, the author will, from next Monday, have the authority to puzzle you by accidentally liking a photo on your Facebook page from 2010 when he was having a snoop to see who you ended up marrying.'

Fanning the flames of a local controversy

You know the scenario. There's been a row locally. Maybe the Tidy Towns chairperson found a few envelopes, bearing the address of a local resident, stuffed in a bag and dumped over the wall at the local pitch and, in an ill-advised move, decided to put photos up on Facebook.

If you want to really get the tempers going, it'll be something involving children. Maybe an unruly child excluded from a school tour.

In a non-social media world, when people had to communicate face to face, these rows would have been muttered at the back of mass, in the shop while getting the paper or down the pub, but would have fizzled out or simmered under the surface like an Indonesian peat forest fire. Perhaps for generations. But the catchment area would have been very small and eventually it would have faded into memory.

Now, though, Facebook provides the perfect opportunity to provide a permanent record of local rows. To take part in one of these conflagrations, you just need a few stock phrases. What you don't need are the full facts.

- 'Hes just a child how wud u feel if it was ur child mayb he was miss behavin.'

- 'This needs to be shared all over so that everyone knows what [insert name of authority figure/ organizer] is really like.'

- 'I'm not being bad but . . .' and then proceed to 'be bad'.

- 'Lot of people on here talking bout wat happened but dey weren't dere.'

- 'What would you expect from them? Wasn't the father the same?'

Sometimes a 'well-meaning' person will intervene to cool things off but ends up throwing a metaphorical can of petrol on the flames:

'Guys, guys, let's cool things down a bit. You're all entitled to your opinions, of course, but obviously some people have issues.'

'Wat do u mean issues we hav no issus he is a lovely boy just a bit lively now nd agin anywy u don t know de facts and wen dey come out a lot of peepl on here chatting shit gonna have a wakeup call.'

Even if there's no evidence of race in the debate, nip in and call someone a racist and you'll be surprised what turns up:

'I'm not a racist I jus tink tat we should look after our own first and anyway, I don't know how my rubbish got into that bag.'

How to protect your privacy using the Irish language

Some people show at least a modicum of awareness of privacy settings. A favourite trick in Ireland is to put your Facebook name in Irish so that people can't find you easily, particularly if your job requires a lot of discretion. Because our knowledge of Irish is sketchy, you can get away with adding as many consonants or vowels into your name as you like and most people will assume that's the correct original spelling. Therefore, someone you know as having a normal name can appear as having a name so laden with arcane spelling and extra letters they sound like a figure from Ireland's mythological past, a trusted lieutenant of Queen Maeve (or Medb/Medbh/Meadhbhghrgh) of Connacht, a woman who was said to have induced menstrual pain in the hearts of her opponents just by raising an eyebrow and looking at them quizzically.

So if someone you used to know as Ann Brown suddenly turns up as Maeliosafhoinseach Ni Mhurchadhachasaigh, chances are she's just started studying to be a teacher.

Baiten Up

You swear you won't fall for it again. You've been hurt so many times. But there's *something* about the way the headline is structured. You think 'Maybe I *won't* believe what happened next' or 'Maybe this story about a model and her rugby-playing boyfriend is *more* than a collection of their Instagram photos of their trip to Dubai. Maybe this one *does* have real heart and some lessons that can be applied to my life.'

But you are wrong. All it tells you is that the 'loved-up

couple' are just enjoying life at the moment and not really thinking about planning a family. But they 'would like kids in future'.

Inside you feel a tiny little pinprick of disappointment – a bit like most meringue-eating experiences – to add to all the other times you clicked on something in the hope of learning something new to stave off the realization of the great gaping hole at the heart of modern life. You've fallen once again for clickbait. You are the fish wriggling away with your tongue pierced on a hook consisting of 300 words of nothing, two tweets and a quote from a non-existent friend close to the couple about how 'Jack and Emily are, like, totally head over heels for each other'.

It's clickbait. For those of you who prefer your news presented in a format that is tangible, tuckable under the arm and useful for starting a fire, imagine if your newspaper started giggling or wowing or roaring to itself in the corner of the room and, as you approached, it said, 'Oh, you're going to want to read this.' And then you read it and it was mostly rubbish. And then an hour later it did it again and you fell for it again.

It's not your fault but at the same time, it sort of *is* your fault. It's not your fault in the same way that getting burgled is not your fault. While you are going about your day, arguing with automated checkouts, trying to prevent babies from bumping their heads, standing on the side of the road waiting for breakdown assistance because cars don't have spare wheels any more, there are other people whose job it is to try to get you to want to know about THIS MAN'S AMAZING TRICK TO SPEAK FOURTEEN LANGUAGES.

Teasing the reader is nothing new. Newspapers in the 'offline world' (or 'reality' as it used to be called) will continue a front-page story on page 4 (or pages 2, 3, 4, 5, 6, 15, 16 and 17 in the case of some). Tabloid newspapers do it with large headlines designed to grab the attention at the newsstands. But, to be fair to tabloids, there IS a gangland crime problem and that famous woman at the other end of the telephoto lens WAS wearing a bikini when she was 'cavorting with her new beau'.

Irish mothers could be said to be originators of one type of clickbait. 'You'll never guess who died' is a technique to get us all to extend the phone call. But again, someone *did* die. And maybe it *is* a funeral you should be at.

What's going on now, though, is a tsunami of Bx. It's pointless to complain but you can at least watch out for it so that when you fall for it again, you can add self-recrimination to your disappointment. Here's an incomplete checklist of phrases so that you can exercise some control before you give up your precious clicks. Avoiding headlines containing these phrases could reduce your disappointment by a percentage *that will surprise you.*

- **You really need/you must/you will love/you can't do without.** You already have enough imperative in your life. We have very basic needs – food, shelter, broadband, security, USB charging points. Tell yourself: *I can do without this.*

• **You won't believe what so-and-so looks like now.** It's very natural to fall for this. Clickbait might be new but the urge to see whether someone famous has let themselves go is as old as the hills.

• **What happens next will restore your faith in humanity/you won't believe what happens next.** Just to save you time: what happens next is the homeless man gives the woman back the wallet she dropped. The old person is really good at breakdancing. The multi-millionaire footballer hugs the guy in the wheelchair. The dog cries when its owner returns from the War on Terror. (OK, you're allowed the last one as emotional catharsis, especially if you're an Irish male who hasn't cried at anything else in his life. But the recommended dosage is not to exceed twenty minutes a week.)

• **Watch the reaction ...** Of course there's a reaction – why else is this scene being filmed in the first place? In fact, it's very likely that the entire thing has been staged and the reaction is part of the act. Especially if the scene is shot from several angles and you can see the boom dipping into shot.

- **So-and-so just shut down haters with this frankly genius move/tweet/reply.** For a start, you should file a complaint with . . . I dunno . . . *someone* about the use of the word 'genius' as an adjective, never mind the extreme lowering of the bar of what constitutes genius. Einstein would turn in his grave if he saw how the move/tweet/reply is probably mildly amusing at most. For that matter . . .

- **Anything sports-related with 'hilarious' in the title is not.** Most things are rarely hilarious. This author is rarely hilarious and he's trying full-time. Sports people are rarely hilarious. They are in peak physical condition because they spend most of their time in the gym – where nothing hilarious happened ever, apart from that time the fella was looking at the girl and fell off the treadmill and pretended he was doing press-ups (that was hilarious and you should click here). Sport doesn't lend itself to true hilarity since data scientists, nutrition experts and technologists have eliminated a lot of the uncertainty that is required for hilarity to ensue.

- **Wardrobe malfunction.** It might be a flash of side-boob or perhaps a nipple but . . . really? Do you need to see it that badly? You might as well give your clicks to the porn industry. If nothing else, at least you owe them for most of the advances in internet technology over the last few years. Now, an *actual* wardrobe malfunction – like squeaky hinges or a badly hung door – *that* might be worth seeing, especially if somebody is trapped inside.

• **So-and-so opens up for the first time.** They're not going to open up that much. They hope to be in the spotlight for thirty years so they'll have to spread their revelations over a number of openings, to keep some of the powder dry, as it were. Rarely is there much to surprise us in their opening up. It would be great if Destiny Zebedee and Jack Zackworth opened up about their trauma at finding out they were both actually squirrels but that hasn't happened in years.

• **Most people can't even get 5 out of 10 questions right.** This one is oh so sneaky. They know that there's nothing people love more than thinking they're cleverer than other people. You will get 9 out of 10 in the quiz. So will everyone else. This is like the nightclub opening where *everyone* has been given VIP access. And if everyone's a VIP, no one's a VIP.

• **REVEALED/lifted the lid/exposed.** You already know it. Someone else revealed it earlier. Most revelation is re-revelation. It's now widely recognized that the Book of Revelation was the Bible's clickbait.

That's why it was at the end. If it was at the start you wouldn't have read any further.

• **A wave of outrage led to an online petition**. An online petition needs only 1,000 people to sign it to make the news. It wouldn't be that difficult, for instance, to find 1,000 people to sign a petition to restore chocolate bars to their 1970s sizes.

• **Twitter storm** – one small argument. This article will have 100 words and ten tweets which you probably saw already. Note: Twitter storms are always 'sparked'.

• **Slammed** – mildly criticized, possibly indirectly.

• **17 signs you grew up in the 80s/90s/00s or whatever decade the article's advertising is aimed at.** A harmless list of pictures with optional words attached. The only problem is: are we spending too much time on nostalgia to create anything new?

Signs You Grew Up In The 2010s

Your grandparents reading the paper, sighing at things that happened when they grew up in the 1970s.

Your parents spent time looking at lists of 'Signs you grew up in the 1990s' and giggling as they remembered that they too had a Tamagotchi.

Every adult you knew spent time looking at lists of 'Signs you grew up Irish'.

We brought this on ourselves. We used to be happy enough to pay for the paper. You met a real person in the shop who said, 'Not a bad day for it', and you replied that there was 'rain on the way' and you bought the milk and the paper because the paper was a real thing and you didn't mind paying for it. Now, though, you think you can get it for free so the only way the news organization will make money is when you click on the link. And they can only make you click on the link by getting you addicted, by lacing the headline with clicotine.

Sure, some papers will try to make you pay for it but you'll just read the same story that was copied off them by another crowd. Which is why you're reading this book. The cover probably got you interested. And now you're feeling tiny disappointments.

13

Opinion Ate It

SIMILAR TO SPORTS COVERAGE, due to the current limitations in the space–time fabric, only a finite amount of stuff actually happens. So the rest of the time is given over to opinion. Opinion is self-perpetuating as each opinion will generate the one after it, so you could get maybe ten opinions for one actual event.

Giving It a Lash

The best way to summarize opinion is to look at the Backlash cycle.

Lash

For this we will need one person to be the Victim Of A Bad Thing or Person. In a 4,000-word Facebook open letter they outline the Bad Experience.

This gets picked up by the mainstream media. The Victim Of A Bad Thing may get *The Late Late Show* out of it. It looks like, for the moment at least, public opinion is with them. There is a wave of sympathy and all the columnists so far are on their side. This Is All That Is Wrong With Ireland, say the columnists.

Backlash

But wait! Opinionator X, under the headline 'It's Not As Simple As We Think', says that we are too quick to be offended in this society, that while the Bad Thing or Person must have been very distressing for the Victim, they share at least some of the responsibility. When Opinionator X was a younger man/woman something similar happened and they got over it.

They are hailed as brave for daring to speak out against the PC consensus. They should get at least two radio interviews out of it and it may help with their book, *Shooting from the Lip or the Hip*, due out in the autumn.

Backlash to the backlash

Under the headline 'This Is Exactly Why We Have a Problem With Privilege', Opinionator X is lashed for not checking their white cisgender privilege (or one from a list of other privileges that we've only found out about: wealth, being from Cork, not being from Cork, having children, not having children, not having hayfever, having hair) and for Something-shaming.

Gobshite

A Gobshite will enter the fray with a death threat. This person is no more capable of carrying out this threat than a wet J-cloth. They are soon found to have 'issues' and appear in court with a jumper over their head before being released, pending the production of a psychiatric report. And it turns out they were the same person who was arrested that time during That Referendum.

Backlash to the backlash to the backlash

Opinionator X says this is a symptom of society's failure as a whole. And possibly the nanny state. Or the state of the nannies. Also, 'It's getting so that the only group it's OK not to offend is the middle-aged, white, straight male. Who's going to stand up for our rights?'

Measured piece

Someone writes a measured piece under the headline 'What Does The Debate Around The Thing That Happened Say About Debate In Ireland Today?'. They say 'On the one hand' and 'On the other hand'. They finish with 'But one thing's for certain', before going on to state the bleeding obvious.

Retrospective

Someone writes a retrospective piece about how 'A Year Has Passed And What's Changed?'.

List

A few years later, the incident appears in a list of '10 Ways In Which 2016 Was Your Life'.

And that's the media.

How to Debate Online

When the robots have taken over all the worthwhile work and the only career options open to humans are as influencers and Instacelebs, you may feel without purpose. There may come a time when the only thing you have left to do is argue online with strangers about things you've no control over. Here are some handy tips on how to engage in debate online.

1. Don't bother

You really don't have time. This might be the last generation that doesn't have to live with the consequences of climate change, so go out and enjoy the weather. Your parents are getting old; go and visit them. Do you really want to waste precious family time being called *libtard* by an online persona called

@deeznuts7777 whose avatar is their misspelled tattoo? Of course, because you're reading this book, chances are you're a mostly sound person with impeccable taste, who can appreciate that the world is complicated and nuanced and can't be boiled down to 100-word opinions on topics outside of your expertise. You are not cut out for debating with the kinds of people who are very angry. And because you don't know @deeznuts7777, @unitedtillidie5678 or @drillakillaHaHa, you'll never find out why they are angry. You won't be able to understand their motives and therefore you won't feel any empathy. You'll just end up getting angry at them. They could be angry for a number of reasons:

• The genuine inequalities inherent in society are preventing them, or their loved ones, from achieving their potential or accessing services.

• They are valiant defenders of free speech, and may even suggest that the men of 1916 died so that @madbastard would have the freedom to express his views.

• Or the fact that they were told life was theirs for the taking, they could be whoever they wanted to be and now, three masters degrees later, they're living with their mother, who has just this minute suggested: 'Why don't you go on *First Dates* or something, or make an effort, anyway? And it wouldn't be any harm if you had a wash too.'

But if you must, read on for some other very basic tips.

2. Learn the lingo

There are some terms that are useful to know, if not necessarily to use.

- **SHAME (ON)**. Usually, the government, the Minister, the guards, the parents, the youth of today are prime candidates, who should feel the shame that has been cast up on them by @debshunreal1982 in her comment. However, they rarely do feel it to a sufficient degree. This could lead them to having 'some neck on them'.

- **(It's a) Disgrace**. Everything is a disgrace and 'they' should be ashamed (see above). Other useful terms include 'crying shame', 'in this day and age' and 'It's like a third-world country'.

- Since everything is so **PC** these days, 'political correctness' as a phrase seems almost quaint, like someone using a SodaStream unironically or your grandmother saying, 'I suppose that's what you'd call "trendy" now.' It is grammatically incorrect to write 'PC' without using quotation marks. 'PC' is like Health and Safety – there to stop normal, honest-to-goodness people from going about their business. If you're 'PC', you're probably also a 'bleeding-heart liberal'. Bleeding-heart liberals want Netflix and *premium* Spotify subscriptions as mandatory benefits for the two or three criminals who are somehow jailed despite the bleeding-heart liberal bail system.

• If you're a bleeding-heart liberal or maybe have religious beliefs but are not that 'protesty', chances are you're one of the **sheeple**. The sheeple are the majority of the population who can't SEE WHAT'S GOING ON IN FRONT OF THEIR FACE. The sheeple are sleepwalking – or shleepwalking – to their own executions unless they pay heed to internet commenters such as dessiebeans45. Whether it's the Military-Industrial Complex/Establishment/Blueshirts/Fianna Fáil Galway Races tent/intelligentsia/commentariat/Opus Dei/the crowd that make all the fizzy drinks/chem trails manufacturers, Dessie777 has their number. The man was clearly sent here to warn us of our ovinity.

• **SJW**. You will see this scattered around and initially might think it has something to do with the Jesuits. It stands for Social Justice Warrior. Used correctly, it describes a particularly unctuous breed of bandwagon-jumpers, who post comments on whatever is the fashionable topic of the day. Used incorrectly, it means 'anyone who is trying to show even a smidge of humanity towards others'.

245

• **Splaining** is a new suffix derived from the word 'explaining' but the 'ex' has been lopped off and replaced with a number of other words according to the context. (That previous sentence, for instance, could be called 'wordsplaining' or perhaps just 'explaining'.) Splaining is explaining someone else's experience to them. The most common is the original mansplaining, as in 'Thank you for mansplaining that to me'. Technically, splaining should only be used as an insult if the splainer – say, for example, a man – is telling the splainee about something the splainee has direct experience, and therefore greater knowledge, of – such as being a woman.

Other forms include whitesplaining and straight-splaining. Sprainsplaining is another one (which I've just made up) and involves empathizing with someone suffering from an injury, such as a broken leg, by telling them how you sprained your ankle once. Finally, there's doublesplaining – where a third party tries to interject to say the person is splaining, but ends up in a splainatory position themselves. A good tip for splainers: do it in a book. By the time it comes out you'll have moved on with your life and therefore can legitimately say, 'Actually, I was a different person back then', and if they challenge you on that, just say, 'Oh, thank you for colmsplaining how I was *really* feeling back then.'

The inherent catch-22 with splaining is that it can be used as a way of defending someone who is just plain wrong. But be very careful. If you are a male arguing with a woman online and you say 'I'm not mansplaining, you're just talking rubbish', you're not going to win.

3. Look them up

Sometimes it can be unnerving dealing with strangers online. But not all are anonymous. The person accusing you of being a sheeperson is a real human being and, if it's Facebook, it can be comforting to see their Facebook page and a lovely photo of them with their family, along with an inspirational saying. Take note of this, but don't say in your reply to them that they have a lovely family because it looks like you are threatening them.

4. Know when to quit

There are many opportunities to quit, such as at the very start of the row, but one good checkpoint is: are they spraying BLOCK CAPITALS THROUGHOUT THEIR ANSWER? Unless they're like your grandmother when she first got her phone and couldn't switch the caps off, chances are they're shouting. You can't outshout them. There are no bigger block capitals.

5. Don't agree to disagree

They're wrong. Let them wallow in their wrongness. You need to go and get a choc-ice.

6. Just for kicks, bring up somebody who had the right idea

Bail laws too lax? Children lacking all respect? Political correctness gone mad. There's only one solution – a list of foreign lads or lads from the past who had the right idea to put manners on the feckless. These include:

- **The Saudis**. Who'd chop your hand off for stealing and that would be the end of it, I'd say.

- **The Russians**. Stalin, right? The Kulaks or wan a them crowds stood up to him and he just killed them all or shipped them off to China or somewhere. No messin' at all.

- **The Singaporeans**. They'll whip you with a sally rod if you drop chewing gum on the ground.

- **The Americans**. Did you see the way they went after them bankers (probably only the once)? If Bernie Madoff was in Ireland, he'd be a minister, HAH?

- **Genghis Khan**. You wouldn't see Genghis Khan announcing a 'consultation period'. He'd be straight out the door, making a pyramid of the skulls of his enemies. That'd be all the consulting he'd do.

- **[Insert dictator/strongman's name]**. He needed to build a railway and he just built it. None of your environmental-impact assessment shite with that fella. And say what you like about Trump, but what's so wrong with a wall?

While this form of reaction to bolloxology can be satisfying in the short-term, it is of no use and ultimately won't fix what's really annoying you. And Stalin wouldn't have given you the planning permission for the extension any quicker either.

Nazi spies everywhere

The online population is becoming increasingly militarized. No shots have been fired yet but if you are to believe some, the armies are already mustered. Battlefield experts have identified the following formations:

- **PC Brigade** – the worst kind. If there is so much as a sniff of a discussion about racism, sexism, homophobia, transphobia, classism and any other -isms or phobias, the PC Brigade will be ready to go with their 'statistics and facts' to counter the gut feelings of straight-talking god-fearing tax-payers.

- **Gay Brigade** – a particularly flamboyantly dressed army fighting for compulsory gayness and moisturising.

- **Nazis** – a broad category that includes *Feminazis* (feminists who are also actual Nazis); the *Breastapo* (a group of women who believe in feeding children using their breasts in public but are also a murderous police force in secret); and *Grammar Nazis* (people who believe in enforcing grammar rules and liquidating those who say 'tat' instead of 'that' and 'should of' instead of 'should have'). This group is said to have the most support among the general population.

- Civilian versions of the above include the *PC Lobby* and the *Gay Lobby*. It's not clear who they are lobbying but they are actively up to something in order to further the PC Agenda and the Gay Agenda. These Agendas may do more to bring about the end of days than any brigades or Nazis.

U OK HUN?

Attila ya later.

How to Write to the *Irish Times*

Sometimes with all this social media and internet commenting, we forget the old ways of doing things. *The Irish Times* letter writer is almost an artisan at this stage.

Sir,

I note with interest that . . .
[Two recent events have occurred that are unconnected but the letter-writer will attempt to connect them. Most of the time, the connection will be tenuous but sometimes the Letter-writing Gods will just hand it to them on a plate. Examples that will have the letter writer creaming themselves include:

- *A gas leak near the Dáil*
- *Infestation of mice or rats near the Dáil*
- *Anything PLUS the Dáil]*

Does this mean now that *[insert outlandish conclusion]*?
Or are we going to see *[insert crap pun]*?

Yours, etc.,

Tiernan O'Scrudaitheoir,
Chortling Away In My Golf Jumper,
Terenure *[They could be from anywhere but it's most likely Terenure.]*

14

Counselling Required

IN FUTURE, WE MAY REACH a point where we have dealt with many mental-health issues, but social media is cooking up a whole new suite of melancholy for us to tackle. Specialized social media counsellors will be required for a number of situations.

The Tweet that Didn't Land

It's a common situation. A televisual event is taking place that, for a while at least, engages a large audience. It could be an election leader's debate, a Toy Show, Eurovision, the Boys In Green Doing Us Proud or a properly famous person on *The Late Late Show*, famous enough for the chattering classes to switch over from Graham Norton.

The twitterati are primed. Someone else has got in early with a zinger. Your turn.

Colm O'Regan @colmoregan · 16s
Something something Irish Water something something, haha #hashtag #lmao!

You send it and wait for the approbation. And wait. Nothing. Maybe the internet is down. Check another website. It's working fine. Wait! There's one notification. Here it starts now. Ah FECK IT! It's just one of those automatic Twitter accounts that has used your tweet as an excuse to introduce their boobs and bottom to you.

Was it something you said? Or didn't say? Maybe you're not famous enough. Maybe it was jealousy. Refresh the page again or drag your thumb down your iWhatsit screen. No, still nothing. All around you friends, strangers, enemies are liking and retweeting other people's stuff. Yet nothing for you.

Your words hang there like a banner in a function room decorated for a birthday party that no one attended while the shouts of people enjoying themselves in the main bar can clearly be heard.

How do you deal with this ennui? Talk to someone. And also maybe delete the tweet and move on. You don't want everyone to see that no one saw.

No Likey for Poor You

A friend has put up a photo of their baby on Facebook. Some people put up so many photos of their babies that if you clicked through their album quickly enough, it would make one of those speeded-up videos of the child growing up.

Excessive baby-photo posting is like issuing too many shares in a company. The value is diluted. If, however, the poster is reasonably restrained, people might actually want to see the photo, so a lot of likes and comments ensue.

You could just comment 'Lovely' and leave it at that. You'll get an appreciative thank-you like from one of the parents. The Facebook equivalent of a brief nod. If you're male, you can get away with some sort of good-natured 'banter' with the father. 'Gorgeous baby. Is that your child at all? Haha.' Or something like: 'As a parent I can tell you that the best is yet to come :/'

But you may not be able to resist adding a bit more personality to your comment. Something that implies you have a bantertastic relationship with the parents. 'There'll be no snorting tequila now for ye', perhaps, or 'Haha, is that a new couch? It won't be long before all your nice furniture is completely destroyed by the children. Ah, the single life is over now, haha lol.'

Before you do, though, consider the following questions:

- Are you a 'character'?

- Have you done this before?

- Are you *actually* friends with the parents or have you just been suggested to them via a complex and sometimes malfunctioning Facebook algorithm that also suggested you should be friends with Nutribullet and a Turkish hip-hop artist?

- What's the comment preceding yours? Is it an aunt who has just written: 'The blessings of Saint Térèse of the Little Flower on ye all'?

Typically, what will happen is that the baby-owner, having wallowed in the rush of all those notifications, will then do a spot of housekeeping and like all of the individual comments. Except yours. All those little blue thumbs and nothing next to yours except the invisible wagging finger of a community wondering who yer wan/man is.

Viral Children, or Working for the Mam

The words 'children' and 'viral' in the same sentence have always had significance. Of course, it used not mean that someone was going viral; it was something viral 'going'. 'Children going viral' meant Child A bringing a vomiting bug into the crèche or a similar Bugtopia, leaving a trail of mucus around the place like a hyperactive mutant snail, making a 1,000 per cent Return on Investment on said vomiting bug, and infecting an entire parish.

That hasn't changed. In fairness to actual viruses, they are a useful antidote to bolloxology in general because they 'put a stop to your gallop'. But now the viral child has taken on a new meaning. It's when they do something cute, recorded on camera by their parents and posted online. It gets millions of views or hits or Vine loops or likes or retweets or follows or haterz. The child appears on *The Ellen DeGeneres Show*, is given loads of free stuff and then we wait for the next cute child.

Yes, the world is a richer place for all this footage of small children being cute. There was a time when we poor, benighted viewers, starved of the chance to see a toddler knocked over by a small goat, would have had to wait for an episode of *You've Been Framed*. Even then, the video might have been from deepest whitest America, with a group of people standing around, sporting mullets and guns, who we didn't really identify with. Now, thanks to the internet, we get to see Irish babies being cute on demand.

So what? There is no better antidote to reading about a Dáil kerfuffle, involving a TD being thrown out for raising something that was not on the order of business, than watching a puppy sitting on a dote's head. There's no bolloxology here. The bolloxology arises when we realize it might not be about the children at all, but actually *about the parents.*

If the 'deleted items' folder of parents' phones or tablets is the equivalent of the film industry's cutting-room floor, then it's likely to be filled with hours of

I need to
return this
cat.

Aw. Is she not
settling in?

CAT
ADOPT

It's not that. It's
just her Youtube
videos don't get more
than 50 views!

What?!

CAT
ADOPT

I know! I thought
She'd be a star! So...
got any weird, ugly cats?

CAT
ADOPT

footage of children not being cute but just sitting there doing normal stuff, interspersed with the frustrated off-camera sighs and cajolings of the parents. Studies show that only 0.001 per cent of such footage makes it on to the internet, and only 0.00001 per cent of these recordings could be called virable.

The percentages for cats tend to be even lower. For dogs, though, the success rate is as high as 90 per cent. Because dogs.

But there are parents who 'leverage' cuteness according to one of the basic Laws of the Internet.

My problem + internet = now it's everyone's problem

Problems such as the rash of letters from suspiciously precocious children to large shops requesting some sort of change to store policy. The organization – mindful that this thing could go viral – then writes a 'perfect response'. The parent publishes this online. The internet laps it up. And then you look at the LinkedIn profile of the parent who 'wanted to highlight how the injustice was obvious even to a little child' and it turns out they are a Social Media Knowledge Champion, who is an expert in thought leadership and driving growth in blue-chip organizations through social media engagement.

I wish that, for once, a grumpy functionary deep in the bowels of Globo Toyz or WORLDSHOPZ would write back and say:

> 'Dear kid, the answer is NO. Hopefully, this will be a valuable lesson to you and your attention-seeking parent, who wrote most of the letter, that sometimes you can't have what you want. Count yourself lucky. Our supply chain includes children the same age as you, who work 14 hours a day.'

The irony of this is that family homes are themselves becoming the western world's sweatshops, with children forced to perform for hours at a time for a fee far below the minimum wage (i.e. parental approval), which they are only paid if their product gets past strict quality control (i.e. the approval of the internet).

But what is the long-term effect of all of this viral mania? Will it put pressure on parents to get their children to do something cute? What if the child just sits there? Some children are actively refusing to play along. Today's eight- and nine-year-olds are being asked to pose for so many photos and videos they are actually avoiding parents bearing phones.

Flash in the Pans

You can't be any kind of misanthrope worth your high-sodium, blood-pressure-raising, non-sea salt if you don't get a crestfallen expression on your face at the sight of a flash mob. If you're not familiar with one, a flash-mob video has the following stages*:

1. There are shots of people looking blissfully unaware of what is about to happen. One sunglassed tourist may be eating an ice-cream. A businessman is on the phone. Some other stressed-out office types walk past, clearly trapped in their suits and their jobs, working for The Man.

2. Something's happening! A man who we thought was just another tourist in shorts and a T-shirt bearing the logo of the '1975 Waikiki Surf Tournament Hawaii' turns out to be part of some kind of performance. Could it be . . .? He sings the first line of a song from That Musical.

3. There are puzzled looks from bystanders in the square. What's yer man at, at all? Is he stone mad? But then more people join in the song. They walk slowly towards the centre of wherever they are.

4. It dawns on people what's going on. Yes, it's a flash mob! There are smiles of recognition. Some

---

*This is a description of a flash-mob video, not the experience of an actual flash mob. This is because a flash mob – similar to a tree falling in the forest – is not deemed to have taken place if it hasn't been recorded, uploaded to the internet, gone viral and tempted you away from that spreadsheet, using the enticing headline 'It Looked Like A Normal Day At The Airport And Then THIS Happened'.

people start filming. Those who are seen to mouth 'Ah for f*ck's sake, a flash mob' are edited out of the video, as are the uncoordinated people who try to join in.

If you're the type of person who gets annoyed by flash mobs, it is unlikely you will ever be part of one, so your only fear is that one will materialize around you. The important thing to remember is that, as far as we know, they don't actually cause any harm to you in the long term. It is possible that prolonged exposure to flash mobs could lead to trust issues because you expect every humdrum situation to explode into *The Lion King* at any moment. But we don't know. They haven't been around long enough for studies to be conclusive. But you can't trust studies either (see page 34).

Some places don't tolerate them at all. Russian police are investigating a No-Pants Subway Ride in Moscow earlier this year. You do have to admire the Russians' strong anti-Bx stance (see page 248). Flash mobs may annoy you in the way that surfers annoy you. They're positive, happy people. And you're not part of the gang.

They're worse than surfers, though, because surfers flaunt their health and happiness and positivity out at sea whereas flash mobs are found far inland, often next to you. And they're exclusive because this was something that was clearly planned without consulting you. Every cast of a musical returning home on public

I'm taking part in a FLASH MOB

What's that?

We meet, we dance, everyone stares at us! Then we act like we don't know each other!

So basically it's like a teenage disco without the shifting?

transport, every 'heart-warming moment' organized in a railway station was designed to catch you on the hop. And you don't like being caught on the hop. You can be as spontaneous as the next fella as long as both you and the next fella have a bit of notice. Let's be honest – flash mobs are enjoyable mostly to the people taking part. They have the secrecy of planning, the coordination, the tension of 'will it be a success?' and the euphoria afterwards. All we get out of it is the vague sense of being used, having to return to our previously humdrum lives, unable to get that feckin' Andrew Lloyd Webber song out of our heads.

In their defence, they do disperse quite quickly, unlike the man with the guitar at the party, who sings all night.

Social Displays of Grieving

It's been a tough year for our past. Singer after movie star after sports star has died and taken with them a chunk of memories. It has also been traumatic for us, the public, as we have been exposed to an unprecedented burst of other people's grief. Typically, the cycle goes as follows:

- The news first breaks.

- People post something on social media, like: 'Oh, no – another part of my childhood gone.'

• Someone posts a video of the dead person's work along with a very detailed explanation of why this person meant so much to them at a pivotal point in their emotional development. The 400-word status update sits there on everyone's timelines and people feel compelled to like or share it because otherwise it's going to look awkward.

• A minor celebrity mentions how they 'had the pleasure of meeting [insert deceased celebrity] once and, you know what, they were so DOWN TO EARTH/NOT OF THIS EARTH'.

• Another celebrity mentions how, while they didn't meet the deceased, they had always been a fan of their work. If this celebrity is currently under a cloud for other reasons, or just genuinely disliked, no one believes they could ever have liked said dead celebrity because knowing that the non-dead disliked celebrity likes someone you love would make it all grubby.

• At no point does anyone in the public eye, when questioned, say, 'Nope, never knew him'.

• There is a petition to immortalize the celebrity on something – maybe a stamp – often qualified by 'far more deserving than [insert other person who has recently been immortalized in this way]'.

• One person misjudges the public mood and voices mild criticism of the dead celebrity. They are subject to a Backlash (see page 240).

• An Important Piece is written in the Important Paper about how Public Grieving is an example of the general narcissism of our times. They will pick a number of events that highlight this and then make a sweeping generalization about all of humanity. (Just like this book does, but that's different.)

• There is a backlash against the Important Piece (beginning, of course, in the below-the-line comments), saying people should be allowed to grieve in whatever way they want, written by someone who had already penned several pieces about how the dead celebrity wasn't just a singer but *all of us.*

• One year later, the celebrity's death will reappear on social media just after the death of someone else and people will think they've only just died.

BLOGGER

VLOGGER

Stop writin' shite
and makin' vidyas and
get ready for Mass!

BOGGER

Bollexicon

Truth Be Told

AKA being honest with you/TBH/being honest with you/not gonna lie/in all honesty/the truth is. In an uncertain world where lies abound, it's important for everyone to be factual. And for them to tell you they're factual. Even where it seems unnecessary: 'Not going to lie, it was roasting warm today.'

Although temperature can be independently verified with a thermometer, you don't know who might be manipulating the figures. Probably climate-change fanatics. Don't tell me any lies – just how warm *was it* today?

Recently 'the truth is' has arrived in from American TV. 'The truth is' usually makes its first appearance at the 35-minute mark in the episode when a character 'doesn't know what to believe any more'. We've started saying it in Ireland but, being honest with you, it just doesn't suit our mouths. It's a thing that people say in the media to buy themselves a few seconds to gather their thoughts. It sounds better than 'Emmmmmm'. 'The truth is', 'let's be clear', 'let's get real' – all mean the same thing. Which is nothing.

Note: 'Honestly' is never used in this way. 'Honestly' is almost exclusively used by mothers over the age of fifty:

- To express surprise at what the world is coming to, at all at all.

- To indicate that something is a 'turn-up for the books'.

'Honest-to-GOODness' will also work here.

A Conversation

The phrase 'happy that I've started a conversation' is an incredibly useful one to get yourself out of a mess. Here's how the conversation starter works:

1. Say or do something stupid or insensitive.

2. Get caught out.

3. Initial defiance (optional). This doesn't always happen but when it does, it always makes matters worse. This could be because you gave an interview on a bank holiday when your publicist/spin doctor was away on a long-deserved golfing break/spa

weekend and didn't have a chance to get to you before you opened your mouth. During this bit you will be seen to be *angrily rubbishing claims* or, in extreme cases, using very simple or straightforward language that can be easily understood. This is exceptionally dangerous because it allows people to see what you are really like.

4. Make a conciliatory statement, which is partly about admitting responsibility but mainly about welcoming the opportunity to have a *national conversation*. Suddenly, it's all our problem. You did the bad thing but actually you were doing us a favour because your actions bravely unveiled the woodlice underneath the national floor mat. Typically, we have a conversation 'around' the topic, which a lot of the time means beating around the bush. Note: a national conversation never really takes place.

5. Get a column in a newspaper where your straight-talking is to be applauded. In fact, you can sneakily row back on the half-apology you made, saying you 'bowed inevitably to the forces of political correctness'.

The Craic

There shouldn't be anything inherently bolloxological about craic, even though its spelling has a whiff of Bx about it. Crack was originally an English and Scottish word but, in a rare episode of cultural appropriation, a gang of Irish rapparees sailed to the UK in a boat and brought the crack back. They may have stopped along the way because the song says 'the *crack* was ninety in the Isle of Man'. Somewhere the spelling changed to 'craic' and the rest is invented history.

For some people, the fact that the spelling has been invented makes them very angry indeed. But people who complain about the spelling of the word are obviously zero craic themselves. Craic has proven very handy in the marketing of Ireland. A trip to Ireland has become synonymous with 'the craic' but the precise definition of how you might witness the craic on your holiday here is never really presented. That's because the craic can be found in any one of the following situations:

- The cheer that goes up when someone drops glasses in the bar.

- A scuffle on the pavement that spills out on to the bonnet of a taxi.

- A trad session which is clearly out of tune but nobody can intervene because the musicians would take fierce offence.

• An oddball carrying an old Dunnes Stores bag and arguing with the bus driver.

Ironically, the most common use of craic is where there has been no craic at all, as witnessed in the following exchanges:

'Well!'

'How're you?'

'Any craic?'

'Ah shur, you know yourself. Any craic with you?'

'F*ck all.'

Or:

'How was last night?'

'Ah it was . . . grand . . . good craic, I suppose.'

It wasn't good craic. The place was too loud and they couldn't get seats and so they ended up leaving but then couldn't agree on where else to go. That was the craic.

Banter

Do you know what's worse than no craic at all? Banter, the modern-day compulsory fun. The successor to craic, it is EVERYWHERE now. Banter used to just mean a bit of light-hearted joshing between friends, now it has expanded to encompass nearly all human interaction, ranging from saying hello to strapping the Stag to a lamp-post, covering him in honey and setting killer-bees on him. The next time a judge hears 'just a bit of banter that got out of hand' used as an excuse, he should sentence the defendant to ten years' hard banter.

Super

As an adjective, most of the time 'super' just means 'very' or even 'quite' or possibly just 'at normal levels'. There was nothing wrong with 'very'. It's a veritable stalwart (*see* Veritable). Inflation of 'super' means that a superman is now just a great guy, pretty sound, not a bollox, rather than a hero. Superman himself would probably be a legend, as long as he's up for the banter (*see* Banter).

Veritable

Previously for exclusive use with 'smorgasbord' or 'treasure trove' or 'Garden of Delights', this is now a word that is the veritable epitome of a superfluity.

Existential-ISm

'It is what it is.' No, just stop that. You were brought on the radio panel to talk about what it is. 'It is what it is' is not an answer, unless you're God (I am who I am), Gloria Gaynor ('I Am What I Am') or Popeye (I yam what I yam). WHAT IS IT? Describe it. Is it a cat? Does it have a colour? Another variant on this is 'We are where we are'. Unless you have a Masters in Bilocation or Time Travel, just don't say this.

Similarly, maybe we could cut back on 'How long is a piece of string?' I don't know, why don't you measure it? If you don't have a tape, guess, or use your feet and then measure your feet afterwards.

Commercially Sensitive

There are few phrases that inspire more rage in a battered people than 'commercially sensitive'. It translates loosely as 'we can't tell you how much yer man offered/got paid/tendered for'. That's probably fair enough if it was you and you didn't want the whole parish to know what you were earning in case they'd have you plagued to sponsor the local team. But it has been used for the past seven years as a reason why Official Ireland can't tell you why The Stupid Thing was done.

It's the political version of 'That's the why', the Irish Mammy staple for when she is too tired or too busy to explain and anyway, if you don't put on your coat we'll all miss the train; and she at least was probably right anyway. The government, on the other hand, more often than not doesn't want to tell you they were wrong.

'Commercially sensitive' can be used in any of the following situations:

- Why we don't stand up to banks.

- What the f*ck NAMA is up to.

- Why they spent so much on that thing when someone else offered to do it for half the price.

- How many tickets did we get and where are they now?

When you hear 'commercially sensitive', take it that it's a sore topic and stay away from it or you'll get a solicitor's letter. Then some foreign journalist or police force who don't give a hoot about commercial sensitivities will blow the lid off the thing and we find out it mightn't have been commercially sensitive at all, but *politically* sensitive. Or shnakey.

It Didn't Do Us a Bit of Harm

From time to time you may be faced with that pillar of Bx – Taking One Example And Extrapolating From It.

This book does plenty of that but this book is allowed because it's called *Bolloxology*.

These examples include:

• The man who smoked sixty fags a day – unfiltered Sweet Afton – and lived till he was ninety-four.

• We could drive home with a few pints on us and no one got hurt.

• Don't mind that Food Safety Crowd. I never got sick eating reheated chicken in my life. And I was eating chicken before you were knee-high to a duck.

Many of these claims hark back to an Ireland that may or may not have existed before 1980. They usually finish with the phrase ' . . . and it didn't do us a bit of harm'. Mass twice a day, regular beatings, a broken stick as a Christmas present and none of yer oul 'rights'.

Of course, the response to that should be: 'You're emotionally repressed, you're not speaking to your sister, you raised a family of functioning alcoholics and you allowed the Catholic Church and a few of the other professional classes to oppress the people worse than the Brits ever did . . . So, yes, it did do you a bit of harm.' But most of us are still too repressed or polite to say this.

Literally

Or LITrally for short. Lookit, we might as well admit defeat but not before one last scream into the void. 'Literally' means exactly what happened. You didn't 'literally die'. If you did, you couldn't have told us about it unless you were 'literally, like a ghost'. But it's too late. Some dictionaries have included 'Not literally' as a definition for 'Literally'. That's it now. Words can mean whatever you want them to mean. It's completely mackerel, but what can we do except accept it and move on.

Acknowledgements

Thanks firstly to Brian Langan and Eoin McHugh, my publishers at Transworld Ireland. This book took a while to 'find itself', 'figure out who it really was and what its passion was', and the two lads helped cajole, encourage and c'mon-wouldja it into existence. Also to Fiona Murphy, Brian Walker, Sophie Smyth, Rebecca Wright, Katrina Whone, Phil Lord and Andy Allen for all their work in turning scraps of MS Word into a fine-looking book.

Thanks to illustrator Maria Boyle AKA Twisted-doodles – a very talented, funny and perceptive chronicler of life who took some of my half-baked ideas and Mary Berryed them. She also wisely ignored other ideas and came up with something far better.

Thanks once again to Faith O'Grady and all at Lisa Richards for being calming and professional guides taking care of business so that I could concentrate on procrastinating.

For my wife Marie, whose love and invaluable support I could not have done without. I love you and thanks for doing most of the minding of our lovely new daughter which meant I had more time to work on this.

For Ruby, our new family thought leader and driver of change, whose perfect comic timing and lack of toleration of notions keeps manners on me.

For my mother, who had a rough oul year and a bit but whose positivity, good wishes, support and love were like multi-vitamins for me.

Finally, thanks to my father, the late Patrick O'Regan, a man with heroically low levels of Bx but what was there was definitely at the divilment end of the spectrum. I miss you, Dada.

Colm O'Regan is a critically acclaimed stand-up comedian, columnist and broadcaster. He writes a weekly column for the *Irish Examiner* and has written for national online and papery publications on both sides of the Irish Sea. Colm is also a columnist with RTE Radio 1's *Drivetime*, BBC World Service's *In the Balance* and BBC World News' *Talking Business*. He has also written and presented two half-hours of comedy for Radio 1 with more to follow next year. As a stand-up comedian, he has performed all over the world. His stand-up has also featured on RTÉ's *Late Late Show* and on Comedy Central. Colm also set up and runs the @irishmammies Twitter account which, with over 210,000 followers, was the inspiration behind his previous three bestselling books of Irish Mammies. Although where he went with the *language*, I don't know. From Dripsey in County Cork, Colm now lives in Dublin but he's up and down that road a good bit.

Maria Boyle is an illustrator living in Dublin. She is better known as Twisteddoodles, under which name she draws reasonably popular cartoons. She feels awkward when people introduce her to strangers as Twisteddoodles and they have no idea who she is. She now shows them this bio.